Wine Country

A Literary Companion

Edited by Benjamin Russack

Heyday Books
Berkeley, California

Library of Congress Cataloging-in-Publication Data

Wine country : a literary companion / edited by Benjamin Russack.
      p.   cm.
ISBN 1-890771-10-4 (pbk.)
1. Sonoma County (Calif.)—Literary collections. 2. Wine and wine making—
California—Sonoma County—Literary collections. 3. Wine and wine making—
California—Napa Valley—Literary collections. 4. Wine and wine making—
California—Sonoma County—History. 5. Wine and wine making—California—
Napa Valley—History. 6. Napa Valley (Calif.)—Literary collections. 7. American
literature—California. 8. Sonoma Valley (Calif.)—History. 9. Napa Valley
(Calif.)—History. I. Russack, Benjamin.
PS571.C2W64 1998
810.8'0979498—dc21
                                                                98-40387
                                                                CIP

Cover Art: Nancy Willis, "Late Summer"
Cover Design: Rebecca LeGates and Raina Rippel
Interior Design/Typesetting: Rebecca LeGates
Editing: Julianna Fleming
Editorial Assistant: Simone Scott
Printing and Binding: Publishers Press, Salt Lake City, UT

Orders, inquiries, and correspondence should be addressed to:
Heyday Books
P. O. Box 9145, Berkeley, CA 94709
510/549-3564, Fax 510/549-1889
heyday@heydaybooks.com

Printed in the United States of America

10 9 8 7 6 5 4 3 2 1

Contents

Acknowledgments

M any people contributed their hard work and talents to this book. Special thanks to Benjamin Russack, who set out to see what could be gathered and whose finds form the foundation for this collection; Rebecca LeGates for her elegant cover and interior designs; Raina Rippel for contributing design ideas and experience; Simone Scott for help with editing, research, and proofing; Alex Walker, Caroline Knapp, and Amy Arnett for research and production assistance; Nancy Willis for the cover art, as well as leads on contemporary writers to include; Joyce Jenkins, Leonore Wilson, and Earl Thollander for their thoughtful suggestions; the staffs at the Napa Public Library, Bancroft Library, and Berkeley Public Library; Steve Dickison and Small Press Distribution for help in locating numerous titles; and the local writers' groups in the Wine Country for their interest and support. I want especially to thank Julianna Fleming who, as managing editor of this project, brought the many people and pieces together, did the final selection and arrangement, and to whose intelligence and good taste this anthology owes its being.

Malcolm Margolin
Publisher

Introduction

The Napa and Sonoma valleys—collectively known as the Wine Country—comprise the most famous wine-growing region in the United States, its long history very much intertwined with the vines and tendrils of the grapes that grow here.

When the Wappo and Pomo Indians settled this favored area more than four thousand years ago, they found lush growths of the wild California grape (*Vitis californica*), thick vines heavy with fruit that festooned trees along virtually every river and stream. While these earliest inhabitants did not ferment grapes into wine, they valued the vines for cordage and enjoyed the fruits seasonally as well. The area's first gourmets, they noticed that those vines that grow on laurel and willow trees produce tart fruit, while those that grow on white or black oaks produce sweeter fruit. An early observer, V.K.

Chesnut, commented that this was probably due to the fact that those growing on oaks tended to enjoy drier and more open situations.

In 1823, Mission San Francisco Solano was established in what is now the town of Sonoma, the last and northernmost in the chain of twenty-one California missions. Soon after casting the first adobe bricks and cobbling together the first temporary buildings, the Franciscan friars turned their attention to the planting of grapes—the so-called Mission or Criolla variety—to provide them with sacramental wine, and not incidentally with much-needed cheer and comfort as they toiled in this most remote of all European outposts, among people whom they would never fully convert and, indeed, never really understand.

In 1833, Mariano Guadalupe Vallejo, commander of the presidio at San Francisco, arrived in Sonoma to become *administrador* of the newly secularized mission. He had been assigned here by the Mexican government to establish a military presence on the *frontera,* both to safeguard Alta California from encroachments by the Russians and to protect it from raids by hostile Indians who lived beyond the fringes of the "civilized" world. While constructing a huge house, fort, and barracks in Sonoma, he greatly extended the planting of grape vines. In 1838, George C. Yount, a fur trapper born in North Carolina, settled in what is now called Yountville, borrowing cuttings from General Vallejo to create the first cultivated vineyards in the Napa Valley.

Modern grape varieties were brought to this area by Agoston Haraszthy, a Hungarian immigrant, who founded his Sonoma winery, Buena Vista, in 1856. He first planted Zinfandel and Tokay grapes from his native country, and over the next decade introduced many other European varieties as well. By the end of the 1860s, winemaking was flourishing, and the Napa and Sonoma valleys had established themselves as one of the major centers of viticulture in America.

Unlike other agricultural communities, Wine Country, throughout its history, has been a place that stirs the imagination. The weather conditions and topography necessary to create the best wine grapes—well-drained valleys and hillsides, a moderate climate—are the very conditions that humans find "idyllic." Also, fine winemaking seems to discourage large corporate farms and gigantic agri-business manufacturing plants, fostering instead smaller enterprises, often of great individuality and charm. Finally, wine is associated with pleasure, and the appreciation of fine wines is synonymous with sophistication and elegance. Perhaps it is the combination of these elements—the beauty of the landscape, the beneficence of the climate, the charm and individuality of the vineyards and wineries, and the pleasures inherent in wine itself—that have conspired to make Wine Country a tourist mecca. Over 4 million visitors come each year to sample its wines, tour its vineyards, dine in its gourmet restaurants, shop in its stylish boutiques, enjoy balloon rides and bike tours, soak in its spas, and then, at the end of a long day of indulgence, bed down in one of its many posh inns or cozy guest houses.

Yet it would be a mistake to dismiss Wine Country as a mere Pleasure Palace, an assemblage of precious wineries and a playground for adults. Wine Country is also a place where people live and work and raise their children, where they have dreams that are only sometimes realized. It is a place with a surprising history and a social diversity that is not always apparent at first sight. The stories in this collection tell of the Indians who lived here for thousands of years, of the Chinese who once worked the vineyards until they were excluded, of the inmates at the state asylum in Napa, of the drifters and others—not readily visible but still and essential part of the region. If Wine Country seems like the "promised land," perhaps we might do well to remember Christopher Isherwood's stunning statement about California: "California," he said, "is a tragic country, like Palestine, like all promised lands." Amidst the undeniable beauty there is an element of the tragic here—a paradise lost, or maybe never quite attained.

Yet how exasperatingly close to paradise it can be!

Arranged more or less chronologically, the stories, reminiscences, and poems in this anthology pay heartfelt tribute to the remarkable beauty of Wine Country. Some writers, like Robert Louis Stevenson and Jessamyn West, exult in it; singing the praises of the world has long been an essential function of literature.

But literature has other functions as well—to probe and question, to mourn and challenge, to record history and spin fantasy. The selections in this anthology do all of that, and while each piece was chosen for its unique literary or historic value, we hope that this anthology adds up to something more than just a collection of individual pieces of merit. Specifically, we hope that this gathering of writings contributes to a deeper understanding and a richer, more earthy, more humane appreciation of Wine Country—its land, its people, its history, and (yes!) its undeniable and remarkable beauty.

To the Wappo Indians the word *napa* meant, among other things, "bounteous place," or more simply put, "plenty." It is the purpose of this collection to present from a literary perspective not just a simple, one-note story, but a sampling of the real bountifulness and plenty of Wine Country.

Wine Country

Creation Story

Wappo Indians

The place where they lived was flooded. Coyote hid in a hole carved into a rock, along with his grandson Chicken-hawk. After twenty days had elapsed, the water disappeared, and Coyote came out of hiding. He looked around, but there was no one there.

"What are we going to do, grandfather?" asked Chicken-hawk.

"Tsoia'o, tsoia'o," said Coyote, "we'll create people."

He built a sweat-house and gathered feathers, which he placed inside it, one by one. "May these feathers become people!" he said, and the feathers came alive.

The next day, the people awoke but remained lying down and did not speak.

"Grandfather," said Chicken-hawk, "what is the matter with them? They don't talk."

"Tsoia'o," said Coyote, and he went to Old Man Moon.

This version was told by Joe McCloud to linguist Paul Radin in 1918. McCloud, born in the mid-1850s near Napa and married to a Wappo woman, dictated the story in the Wappo language and provided a rough English translation from which this version has been adopted. Wappo Texts *(University of California Publications in American Archaeology and Ethnography, vol. 19, no. 1, Berkeley, 1924).*

"Well?" said Moon.

"I have come seeking words," said Coyote.

Moon placed some words in a sack and tied the end tightly closed. "Here, take it."

Coyote packed the bag on his back and took it to the sweat-house. Once inside, he untied the sack, and the people were able to speak.

The next morning, Chicken-hawk said, "Grandfather, the people are not moving."

"Tsoia'o, tsoia'o," said Coyote, and he went to Old Man Moon again.

"Well?" said Moon.

"I've come for some fleas," said Coyote.

Moon put some fleas in a bag and tied the end tightly closed. "Here."

Coyote packed the bag on his back and took it to the sweat-house. Inside, he opened it and poured out the fleas. They bit the people, and the people started to move.

The next morning, Chicken-hawk said, "Grandfather, they don't laugh."

"Tsoia'o," said Coyote, and he went back to Old Man Moon.

"Well?"

"I've come for some laughter," said Coyote.

Moon put some in a sack and tied the end tightly closed. "Here," said Moon, and Coyote packed the bag on his back and took it to the sweat-house. He opened it up inside, and the people laughed.

That night the people slept, and in the morning, Chicken-hawk said, "Grandfather, the people don't walk."

"Tsoia'o," said Coyote, as he went to Old Man Moon.

"Well?" said Moon.

"I've come after some walking."

"All right," said Moon, and he put some walking in a sack and tied the end tightly closed. "Here."

Coyote took the sack and packed it on his back. He untied it inside the sweat-house, and the people walked.

The next morning, the people walked, laughed, spoke, and moved around.

"Grandfather," said Chicken-hawk, "they don't eat."

"Tsoia'o," said Coyote, and he went to Old Man Moon.

"Well?" said Moon.

"I've come for some bread and acorn mush and pinole," said Coyote.

"All right," said Moon, and he gave Coyote a piece of bread and put some pinole and mush in the bag. "Here."

"Tsoia'o," said Coyote. "Now that's all."

"All right," said Moon. Then Coyote went back to the sweat-house, and when he got there, he divided the bread and pinole and mush, each person getting just enough. The people stayed there and were happy.

✺ The Ghost Dance of 1870

Tolewok was a dreamer at Kelsey Creek. He said the world was going to end and everybody was going to die. They should all come together to die. He thought the world would burn up. The half-breeds were to turn into rocks and stumps. After the end of the world everybody was to come back to life except the half-breeds and the white people. The Indians were not supposed to eat meat or grease. They shouldn't eat white men's food, like hogs, beef, and bread. Mary burned up a new pair of shoes, because they were white people's things.

The Ghost Dance was an apocalyptic religious revival that spread among the Indians of the area at a time of great misery and discouragement. This account was dictated by three Wappo elders—Mary Eli, John Trippo, and Marion Maranda—to anthropologist Cora duBois, who published the material in her monograph, The 1870 Ghost Dance *(University of California Publications, Anthropological Record, vol. 3, no. 1, Berkeley, 1939).*

When the Indians heard this prophecy they came together from all over. All the Wappo from Alexander Valley and elsewhere went, and all the Indians from the coast. They all came together. This was just when the railroad came to Healdsburg [spring, 1872]. At Kelsey Creek there was a large underground sweat-house that had been built. It was different from any seen before. It was so big it could hold about a thousand people. It had a down-sloping corridor entrance oriented eastward, a square smoke hole, and a small rear exit. Around the interior was a raised bench. There was a cottonwood [log] drum in it, and a man played it by dancing on it. The center pole was painted with white clay and had charcoal chevrons painted on it. Outside was a flagpole and a flag with designs in red, white, blue, and black, like a quilt. That was the first flag we had ever seen like that.

In the dance house everyone danced all the time. Tolewok's spirit [ally] told him how everything had to be. His spirit was a ghost [*ote.u*], the spirit of someone who had died. One dancer went out of his mind. He got a song. He sang for Tolewok and worked for him.

But the Indians at Kelsey Creek were starving, and the white people threatened to kill them. So we moved on to Sulphur Bank. At Sulphur Bank everything was fixed up the same way. The white people were afraid because there were so many Indians together. They thought they were going to make war on the whites, so they wouldn't sell the Indians powder and ammunition; but they let them keep their guns. They got some soldiers in.

Meanwhile the Indians made a big sweat-house, maybe twelve feet deep. It would hold two, three, of four thousand people. On the top the *maru* [dreamer] man talked to the people, said the world was coming to an end. Everybody went inside. But nothing happened. This went on day after day. Nothing happened, but the people began to starve and went home. Before going to Kelsey Creek, people had burned everything they couldn't carry, so when we arrived back in Alexander Valley we had nothing.

Voyage to California

Sir George Simpson

At Sonoma—for the very name of the Mission has been secularized—we were received by the firing of a salute and the hoisting of the colors, the former mark of respect being complimentary in proportion to the scarcity of gunpowder in this land of lassos. Through a gateway and a courtyard we ascended a half-finished flight of steps to the principal room of the general's house, being of fifty feet in length and of other dimensions in proportion. Besides being disfigured by the doors of chambers, to which it appeared to be a passage, this apartment was very indifferently furnished, the only tolerable articles upon the bare floor being some gaudy chairs from Oahu, such as the native islanders themselves often make. This was

From An Overland Journey Around the World, During the Years 1841 and 1842. London: H. Colburn, 1847. [A brief biographical note on each author appears in the back matter.]

California all over, the richest and most influential individual in a professedly civilized settlement obliged to borrow the means of sitting from savages who had never seen a white man till two years after San Francisco was colonized by the Spaniards. Here we were received by Don Salvador Vallejo and Mr. Leese, our host's brother and brother-in-law, and immediately afterwards, the general, being somewhat indisposed, received us very courteously in his own chamber.

General Vallejo is a good-looking man of about forty-five years of age, who has risen in the world by his own talent and energy. His father, who was one of the most respectable men in California, died about ten years ago at Monterey, leaving to a large family of sons and daughters little other inheritance than a degree of intelligence and steadiness almost unknown in the country. The patrimonial estate, such as it was, descended to the eldest son, while the second, now the prop of the name, was an ensign in the army, with the command of the Presidio of San Francisco. Having acquired considerable influence in the party which styled itself democratic, and aimed at something like independence, he was promoted by a conciliatory governor to be commandant of the frontier of Sonoma, and soon afterwards, taking advantage of this same governor's death, he became the leader in the revolution of 1836, securing for a nephew of the name of Alvarado the office of civil governor, and reserving to himself the important post of commander of the forces. As to the rest of the family, Don Salvador became a captain of cavalry, and another brother was made *administrador* of the Misión San José, while the girls were married off, most of them to foreigners with a shrewd view to the strengthening of the general's influence....

After spending about half an hour with our host, we left him to partake of a second breakfast, at which we were joined by the ladies of the family. first in honor and in place was Señora Vallejo, whose sister is married to Captain Wilson of the bark *Index,* an honest Scot from "Bonny Dundee"; next came one of her sisters-in-law, who is the wife of Captain Cooper of the schooner *California,* and who resides at

Sonoma as a pledge for the fidelity of the provincial navy; and lastly followed Mrs. Leese with an unmarried sister and Mrs. Cooper's daughter. It won't be the general's fault if the English race does not multiply in California. So far as names went, we might have supposed ourselves to be in London or in Boston.

In front of Mr. Leese, who sat at the head of the table as master of ceremonies, was placed an array of five dishes—two kinds of stewed beef, rice, fowls, and beans. As all the cooking is done in outhouses, for the dwellings, by reason of the mildness of the climate, have no chimneys or fireplaces, the dishes were by no means too hot when put on the table, while by being served out in succession to a party of about twenty people they became each colder than the other before they reached their destinations. It was some consolation to know that the heat must once have been there, for everything had literally been seethed into chips, the beans or *frijoles* in particular having been first boiled and lastly fried, with an intermediate stewing to break the suddenness of the transition. Then every mouthful was poisoned with the everlasting compound of pepper and garlic, and this repast, be it observed, was quite an aristocratic specimen of the kind, for elsewhere we more than once saw, in one and the same dish, beef and tongue and pumpkin and garlic, and potatoes in their jackets, and cabbage and onions and tomatoes and peppers, and heaven knows what besides— this last indefinite ingredient being something more than a mere figure of speech, considering that all the cookery, as one may infer from the expenditure of so much labor, is the work of native drudges, unwashed and uncombed. When to the foregoing sketch are added bad tea and worse wine, the reader has picked up a perfect idea of a Californian breakfast, a Californian dinner, and a Californian supper, and is quite able to estimate the sacrifice which a naturalized John Bull makes for the pleasures of matrimony and the comforts of Roman Catholicism. Such varieties as cheese and butter and milk and mutton and fish are, as I have already mentioned, here unknown. Even game, whether of the land or of the water, is at a discount, not only as a matter of business, but also as an object of amusement; and the very beef has been parboiled in the feverish blood of the unfortunate bullock, first heated and infuriated by the chase, and then tortured and strangled with the lasso.

Immediately after breakfast our horses were brought to the door, and we started to see the country, accompanied by Don Salvador and an escort of three or four soldiers. We first ascended a steep hill at the back of the Mission, whence we obtained an extensive view of the surrounding region. In the distance lay the waters of the magnificent harbor, while at our feet stretched a plain, for it exhibited nothing of the valley but its wall of mountains, about fifteen miles long and three broad. This plain is composed of alluvial soil, which is so fertile as to yield about fifty returns of wheat, and the hills present abundance of willow, poplar, pine, chestnut, and cedar. If one may judge from appearances, this valley once formed an arm of the Bay of San Pablo, and in fact, the whole harbor, in remote ages, was most probably an inland lake which has forced its way to the ocean through the same barrier of soft rock which, as already mentioned, still continues to melt into the tide.

In the course of our ride we saw several deer on the road, these animals being so tame as often to approach the houses in large herds. For beasts of chase, if here the phrase is not a misnomer, California is a perfect paradise. The Californian is too lazy to hunt for amusement, and as to any necessity of the kind, his bullocks supply all his wants, excepting that the red deer is occasionally pursued on account of the peculiar hardness and whiteness of its tallow. Hence the number of wild animals is very considerable. Beaver and otter have recently been caught within half a mile of the Mission, and there are also the red deer, the wild goat, the bear, the panther, the wolf, the fox, the rabbit, etc.

Having descended from the hill, we traversed a great portion of the plain. The waterspout, which has been already mentioned, had done a great deal of damage, sweeping away the newly sown seed from several large fields of wheat. These fields had been highly prized by the general, as the grain had been procured from the Columbia River and was superior in quality to his own. As one might expect from the abundance of land, the fertility of the soil, and the indolence of the people, agriculture is conducted in the rudest possible way. As the surface of the plain presents so few obstacles to cultivation, the same land is never cropped for more than two successive years, and as General Vallejo's farm contains from 500 to 600 acres, he thus annually breaks up about 300 acres of what may be called wild land, either fresh from the hands of nature or refreshed by rest. In the fields that had been stripped by the waterspout, we saw several plows at work, or rather at what expects to be called work in this country. The machine consists of little more than a log of wood pointed with iron, from the top of which rises in a sloping direction a long pole for the oxen, while an upright handle for the plowman is fixed to the unpointed end of the share, or, if possible, is formed out of the same piece of timber as the share itself. The oxen, as if to prevent even them from putting forth their strength, are yoked by the horns, and considering that there are only two such animals to so clumsy a piece of workmanship, the topsoil alone is scratched to a depth of not more than two or three inches....

During the day, we visited a village of General Vallejo's Indians, about 300 in number, who were the most miserable of the race I ever saw, excepting always the slaves of the savages of the northwest coast. Though many of them are well formed and well grown, yet every face bears the impress of poverty and wretchedness, and they are, moreover, a prey to several malignant diseases, among which a hereditary syphilis ranks as the predominant scourge alike of old and young. They are badly clothed, badly lodged, and badly fed. As to clothing, they are pretty nearly in a state of nature; as to lodging, their hovels are made of boughs wattled with bulrushes in the form of beehives, with a hole in the top for a chimney, and with two holes at the bottom, towards the northwest and the southeast, so as to enable the poor creatures, by closing them in turns, to exclude both the prevailing winds; and as to food, they eat the worst bullock's worst joints, with bread of acorns and chestnuts, which are most laboriously and carefully prepared by pounding and rinsing and grinding. Though not so recognized by law, yet they are thralls in all but the name, while, borne to the earth by the toils of civilization superadded to the privations of savage life, they vegetate rather than live, without the wish to enjoy their former pastimes or the skill to resume their former avocations.

This picture, which is a correct likeness not only of General Vallejo's Indians, but of all the civilized aborigines of California, is the only remaining monument of the zeal of the church and the munificence of the state. Nor is the result very different from what ought to have been expected. In a religious point of view, the priests were contented with merely external observances, and even this semblance of Christianity they systematically purchased and rewarded with the good things of this life, their very first step in the forma-tion of a mission having been to barter maize-pottage, by a kind of regular tariff, for an unconscious attendance at church and the repetition of unintelligible catechisms.

With regard, again, to temporal improvement, the priests, instead of establishing each proselyte on a farm of his own, and thus gradually imbuing him with knowledge and industry, penned the whole like cattle and watched them like children, at the very most making them eye-servants through their dread of punishment and their reverence for a master. In truth, the Indians were then the same as now, excepting that they shared more liberally in the fruits of their own labor and possessed spirit enough to enjoy a holiday in the songs and dances of their race. The true tendency of the monkish discipline was displayed by the partial emancipation which took place, as already mentioned, in 1825, and when the missions were confiscated in 1836, the proselytes, almost as naturally as the cattle, were divided among the spoilers, either as menial drudges or as pre-dial serfs, excepting that some of the more independent among them retired to the wilderness, in order, as the sequel will show, to avenge their wrongs by a life of rapine.

These sons and daughters of bondage—many of them too sadly broken in spirit even to marry—are so rapidly diminishing in numbers that they must soon pass away from the land of their fathers, a result which, as it seems uniformly to spring from all the conflicting varieties of civilized agency, is to be ultimately ascribed to the inscrutable wisdom of a mysterious Providence. If anything could render such a state of things more melancholy, it would be the reflection that many of these victims of a hollow civilization must have been born in the missions, inasmuch as, even at San Francisco, those establishments had taken root sixty years before the revolution, and it was truly pitiable to hear Vallejo's beasts of burden speaking the Spanish language, as an evidence that the system, wherever the fault lay, had not failed through want of time.

Previously to dressing for dinner we took a closer survey of the buildings and premises. The general's plan seems to be to throw his principal edifices into the form of a square, or rather of three sides of a square. The center is already filled up with the general's own house, flanked on one side by a barrack and on the other by Don Salvador's residence, but as yet the wings contain respectively only a billiard room and Mr. Leese's dwelling, opposite to each other. On the outside of this square are many detached buildings, such as the *cala-bozo,* the church, etc. The *calabozo* is most probably a part of the original establishment, for every mission had its cage for refractory converts; but the church, which even now is large, has been built by Vallejo to replace a still larger one, though no priest lives at Sonoma, and Father Quijas of San Rafael, after his experience of the dungeon, has but little stomach for officiating at headquarters.

All the buildings are of adobes, or unbaked bricks, which are cemented with mud instead of mortar, and in order to protect such perishable materials from the rain, besides keeping off the rays of the sun, the houses are very neatly finished with verandas and overhanging eaves. If tolerably protected for a time, the walls, which are generally four or five feet thick, become, in a measure, vitrified, and are nearly as durable as stone. To increase the expenditure of labor and materials, the partitions are nearly as thick as the outer walls, each room of any size having its own separate roof, a circumstance which explained what at first surprised us—the great length and breadth of the apartments.

At this season of the year [January] we found the houses very comfortless in consequence of the want of fireplaces, for the warmth of the day only rendered us more sensible of the chilliness of the night. The Californians remedy or mitigate the evil by the ludicrous make-shift of wearing their cloaks, and even among the foreigners not more than two or three dwellings with chimneys will be found from one end of the province to the other.

The garrison of Sonoma is certainly well officered, for the general and the captain have only thirteen troopers under their command, this force and Prado's corps, if they could only get balsas enough to effect a junction, forming a standing army of about twenty men for San Francisco alone. The absurdity of the thing consists not in the number of soldiers, for they are sixteen times more numerous in proportion than the army of the United States. The essential folly is this, that a scattered population of seven thousand men, women, and children should ever think of an independence which must either ruin them for the maintenance of an adequate force or expose them at one and the same time to the horrors of popular anarchy and of military insubordination.

If one may judge from the variety of uniforms, each of the thirteen warriors constitutes his own regiment, one being the "Blues," another the "Buffs," and so on; and as they are all mere boys, this nucleus of a formidable cavalry has at least the merit of being a growing one. The only articles common to the whole of this baker's dozen are an enormous sword, a pair of nascent *mostachos,* deerskin boots, and that everlasting *serape* or blanket with a hole in the middle of it for the head. This troop the general turns to useful account, being clearly of opinion that idleness is the very rust of discipline. He makes them catch his cattle, and, in short, discharge the duty of servants-of-all-work—an example highly worthy of the imitation of all military autocrats. The system, however, has led to two or three revolts. On one occasion a regiment of native infantry, being an awkward squad of fifteen Indians, having conspired against the general, were shot for their pains; and more recently the Californian soldiers, disdaining to drive bullocks, were cashiered on the spot and replaced by new levies. Besides the garrison, the general possesses several field-pieces and carronades, which, however, are, by reason of the low state of the ammunition, rather ornamental than useful.

There is a small vineyard behind the house, of about 300 feet square, which, in the days of the priests, used to yield about 1,000 gallons of wine. The general, on coming into possession, replanted the vines, which bore abundantly in the third season, and now, at the end of only five years, they have just yielded twenty barrels of wine and four of spirits, equal to sixteen more of wine, of fifteen gallons each, or about 540 gallons of wine in all. The peaches and pears also, though only three years old, were from fifteen to twenty feet high, and had borne fruit this season. In short, almost any plant might here be cultivated with success.

During the short winter, snow is never seen, excepting occasionally on the summits of the highest hills, while at noon the heat generally ranges from sixty-five degrees to seventy degrees in the shade, and in summer the average temperature of the day is seldom lower than ninety degrees. As the northwest fogs do not penetrate into the interior more than fifteen miles, there are, in fact, two climates at San Francisco, and General Vallejo has chosen the better one for himself, as also for his brother [Don José de Jesús], the *administrador* of Misión San José.

At dinner the general made his appearance, wrapped in a cloak, and we had now also the pleasure of being introduced to the dowager *señora,* an agreeable dame of about sixty, and we could not help envying the old lady the very rare luxury of being immediately surrounded, at her time of life, by so many as five grown sons and daughters. This meal was merely a counterpart of the breakfast—the same Mr. Leese, the same stews, the same *frijoles,* and the same pepper and garlic, with the same dead-and-alive temperature in every morsel—and the only difference was, that, as we were a little better appetized, we took more notice of the want of attendance, the only servant, besides my own, being a miserable Indian dressed in a shirt, with bare legs and cropped hair.

Immediately after dinner the ladies retired, the gentlemen at the same time going out for a stroll, but soon afterwards the ladies again met us at tea, reinforced by one or two of the more juvenile *doñas* of the establishment. Dancing was now the order of the day. Don Salvador and one of his troopers played the guitar, while we were "toeing it and heeling it" at the fandango, the cotillion, and the waltz. The scene was rather peculiar for a ballroom, both gentlemen and ladies, when not on active service, smoking furiously, with fully more, in some cases, than the usual accompaniments.

Among the persons present was a very fierce, punchy little man enveloped in an immense cloak. He proved to be no less a personage than Commandant Prado of the Presidio of San Francisco, successor, in fact, of Vallejo in the same office which formed the stepping-stone to his present elevation. Besides having been engaged in many skirmishes against both Californians and Indians, he has had several narrow escapes with his life in private brawls. About two years ago a religious festival was celebrated at the Misión San Francisco de Asís in honor of the patron saint, passing through all the usual gradations of mass, bullfight, supper, and ball. In the course of the evening, Don Francisco Guerrero, the steward of the Mission, stabbed Prado with the ever-ready knife for presuming to interpose in an altercation between himself and his mistress; but the corpulent commandant was not to be so easily run through, for though breadth of beam is not generally an advantage to a soldier, yet on this occasion Prado's fat did succeed in saving his bacon. Such a termination of a religious festival is so much a matter of course that at one which took place a few months back one of Prado's numerous enemies came up to him, and, drawing his knife, said, "What! here's daylight, and no one yet stabbed!" and it required all the influence of Vallejo, who happened to be present, to nip so very promising a quarrel in the bud. On such occasions the cloak is often invaluable as a shield, and in fact, when both parties are on their guard, there is commonly far more of noise than of mischief.

Our evening, however, passed over most amicably and agreeably, winding up, after several other songs, with "Auld Lang Syne," in which the Californians joined the foreigners very heartily, so that, as next day was Old Christmas, I could almost have fancied that I was welcoming Auld Yule in the north of Scotland.

On the morning of the sixth we left the Mission about seven o'clock, under a pretty heavy rain, to the great surprise of its amiable and hospitable inmates. We breakfasted at the landing-place, on the site of our old camp, after which we made our way to the mouth of the creek with the ebbtide, but as the wind was blowing hard from the southeast, we could not face the bay, and were obliged to retrace our steps, encamping for the third time at the landing-place, after nearly a whole day's exposure and toil. In all the course of my traveling I never had occasion to go so far in search of an encampment as I did this day, but between our encampment and the bay there really was not a single spot where, even in the direst necessity, we could have obtained a footing. The banks of the creek were a mere marsh, and we saw and heard thousands upon thousands of cranes, geese, ducks, curlew snipe, plover, heron, etc. These birds enjoy a perpetual holiday. They, of course, are quite safe from the lasso, and so long as the Californians can get beef without gunpowder, they are not likely to expend it on any less profitable quarry.

By next morning the wind had returned to the northwest. We accordingly got under way at six o'clock, and, after a pleasant run down the creek, we stood across the Bay of San Pablo, passed our old encampment on Murphy's estate, and at four in the afternoon arrived in safety on board of the *Cowlitz*.

from Phoenixiana

George Horatio Derby

Squibob in Benicia
October 1st, 1850

L eaving the metropolis last evening by the gradually-increasing-in-popularity steamer, *West Point,* I "skeeted" up Pablo Bay with the intention of spending a few days at the world-renowned seaport of Benicia. Our captain (a very pleasant and gentlemanly little fellow, by the way) was named Swift, our passengers were emphatically a fast set, the wind blew like well-watered rose-bushes, and the tide was strong in our favor. All these circumstances tended to impress me with the idea that we were to make a wonderfully quick passage; but, alas, "the race is not always to the Swift," the *Senator* passed us ten miles from the wharf, and it was nine o'clock, and very dark at that, when we were roped in by the side of the "ancient and fishlike" smelling hulk that forms the broad wharf of Benicia.

From Phoenixiana. *New York: D. Appleton and Co., 1855. Originally appeared in the* Pioneer, *San Francisco, 1850.*

As I shouldered my carpet-bag and stepped upon the wharf among the dense crowd of four individuals that were there assembled, and gazing upon the mighty city whose glimmering lights, feebly discernible through the Benician darkness, extended over an area of five acres, an overpowering sense of the grandeur and majesty of the great rival of San Francisco affected me. I felt my own extreme insignificance and was fain to lean upon a pile of watermelons for support. "Boy!" said I, addressing an intelligent specimen of humanity who formed an integral portion of the above-mentioned crowd, "Boy! can you direct me to the best hotel in this city?"—"Ain't but one," responded the youth, "Winn keeps it; right up the hill thar."

Decidedly, thought I, I will go in to Winn, and reshouldering my carpet-bag, I blundered down the ladder, upon a plank footpath leading over an extensive morass in the direction indicated, not noticing, in my abstraction, that I had inadvertently retained within my grasp the melon upon which my hand had rested. "*Saw yer!*" resounded from the wharf as I retired—"*Saw yer!*" repeated several individuals upon the footpath. For an instant my heart beat with violence at the idea of being seen accidentally appropriating so contemptible an affair as a watermelon; but hearing a man with a small white hat and large white mustache shout "Hello!" and immediately rush with frantic violence up the ladder, I comprehended that Sawyer was his proper name, and by no means alluded to me or my proceedings; so slipping the melon in my carpet-bag, I tranquilly resumed my journey.

A short walk brought me to the portal of the best and only hotel in the city, a large two-story building dignified by the title of the "Solano Hotel," where I was graciously received by mine host, who welcomed me to Benicia in the most *winning* manner. After slightly refreshing my inner man with a feeble stimulant and undergoing an introduction to the oldest inhabitant, I calmly seated myself in the bar-room and contemplated with intense interest the progress of a game of billiards between two enterprising citizens; but finding, after a lapse of two hours, that there was no earthly probability of its ever being concluded, I seized a candlestick and retired to my room. Here I discussed my melon with intense relish, and then seeking my couch, essayed to sleep. But, oh! the fleas! skipping, hopping, crawling, biting! "Won't someone establish an agency for the sale of D.L. Charles & Co.'s Fleabane, in Benicia?" I agonizingly shouted, and echo answered through the reverberating halls of the Solano Hotel, "Yes, they won't!" What a night!

But everything must have an end (circles and California gold excepted), and day at last broke over Benicia. Magnificent place! I gazed upon it from the attic window of the Solano Hotel, with feelings too deep for utterance. The sun was rising in its majesty, gilding the redwood shingles of the U.S. storehouses in the distance; seven deserted hulks were riding majestically at anchor in the bay; clotheslines, with their burdens, were flapping in the morning breeze; a man with a wheelbarrow was coming down the street! Everything, in short, spoke of the life, activity, business, and bustle of a great city. But in the midst of the excitement of this scene, an odoriferous smell of beefsteak came, like a holy calm, across my olfactories, and hastily drawing in my *cabeza,* I descended to breakfast. This operation concluded, I took a stroll in company with the oldest inhabitant, from whom I obtained much valuable information (which I hasten to present), and who cheerfully volunteered to accompany me as a guide to the lions of the city.

There are no less than forty-two wooden houses, many of them two stories in height, in this great place—and nearly twelve hundred inhabitants, men, women, and children! There are six grocery, provision, drygoods, auction, commission, and where-you-can-get-almost-any-little-thing-you-want stores, one hotel, one school-house—which is also a *brevet* church—three billiard tables, a post office—from which I actually saw a man get a letter—and a tenpin-alley, where I am told a man once rolled a whole game, paid $1.50 for it, and walked off chuckling. Then there is a "monte bank"—a

Common Council, and a Mayor, who, my guide informed me, was called *"Carne,"* from a singular habit he has of eating roast beef for dinner. But there isn't a tree in all Benicia. "There was one," said the guide, "last year—only four miles from here, but they chopped it down for firewood for the 'post.' Alas! why didn't the woodman spare that tree?" The dwelling of one individual pleased me indescribably— he had painted it a vivid green! Imaginative being. He had evidently tried to fancy it a tree, and in the enjoyment of this sweet illusion, had reclined beneath its grateful shade, secured from the rays of the burning sun, and in the full enjoyment of rural felicity even among the crowded streets of this great metropolis.

How pretty is the map of Benicia! We went to see that, too. It's all laid off in squares and streets, for ever so far, and you can see the pegs stuck in the ground at every corner, only they are not exactly in a line, sometimes; and there is Aspinwall's wharf, where they are building a steamer of iron that looks like a large pan, and Semple Slip, all divided on the map by lines and dots into little lots of incredible value; but just now they are all under water, so no one can tell what they are actually worth. Oh! decidedly Benicia is a great place. "And how much, my dear sir," I modestly inquired of the gentlemanly recorder who displayed the map, "how much may this lot be worth?" and I pointed with my finger at lot number 97, block 16,496— situated, as per map, in the very center of the swamp. "That, sir," replied he with much suavity, "ah! it would be held at about three thousand dollars, I suppose." I shuddered—and retired.

The history of Benicia is singular. The origin of its name as related by the oldest inhabitant is remarkable. I put it right down in my notebook as he spoke and believe it religiously, every word. "Many years ago," said that aged man, "this property was owned by two gentlemen, one of whom, from the extreme candor and ingenuousness of his characer, we will call Simple; the other being distinguished for waggery and a disposition for practical joking, I shall call—as in fact he was familiarly termed in those days—Larkin. While walking over these grounds in company, on one occasion, and being naturally struck by its natural advantages, said Simple to Larkin, 'Why not make a city here, my boy? Have it surveyed into squares, bring up ships, build houses, make it a port of entry, establish depots, sell lots, and knock the center out of Yerba Buena straight?' (Yerba Buena is now San Francisco, reader.) 'Ah!' quoth Larkin with a pleasant grin diffusing itself over his agreeable countenance, 'that would be nice, hey?'" Need we say that the plan was adopted, carried out, proved successful, and Larkin's memorable remark *"be nice, hey,"* being adopted as the name of the growing city, gradually became altered and vulgarized into its present form, Benicia! A curious history, this, which would have delighted Horne Took beyond measure.

Having visited the Masonic Hall, which is really a large and beautiful building, reflecting credit alike on the architect and the fraternity, being by far the best and most convenient hall in the country, I returned to the Solano Hotel, where I was accosted by a gentleman in a blue coat with many buttons, and a sanguinary streak down the leg of his trousers, whom I almost immediately recognized as my old friend, Captain George P. Jambs of the U. S. Artillery, a thorough-going *adobe,* as the Spaniard has it, and a member in high and regular standing of the Dumfudgin Club. He lives in a delightful little cottage, about a quarter of a mile from the center of the city, being on duty at the Post—which is some mile, mile and a half or two miles from that metropolis—and pressed me so earnestly to partake of his hospitality during my short sojourn that I was at last fain to pack up my property, including the remains of the abstracted melon, and in spite of the blandishments of my kind host of the Solano, accompany him to his domicile, which he very appropriately names "Mischief Hall." So here I am installed for a few days, at the expiration of which I shall make a rambling excursion to Sonoma, Napa, and the like, and from whence perhaps you may hear from me.

As I sit here looking from my airy chamber upon the crowds of two or three persons thronging the streets of the great city; as I gaze upon that man carrying home a pound-and-a-half of fresh beef for his dinner; as I listen to the bell of the *Mary* (a Napa steam packet of four cat power) ringing for departure, while her captain in a hoarse voice of authority requests the passengers to "step over the other side, as the larboard paddle-box is under water"; as I view all these unmistakable signs of the growth and prosperity of Benicia, I cannot but wonder at the infatuation of the people of your village, who will persist in their absurd belief that San Francisco will become a place, and do not hesitate to advance the imbecile idea that it may become a successful rival of this city. Nonsense! Oh Lord! At this instant there passed by my window the—prettiest—little—I can't write any more this week; if this takes, I'll try it again.

Yours for ever,
SQUIBOB

Squibob in Sonoma
October 10th, 1850

I arrived at this place some days since, but have been so entirely occupied during the interval, in racing over the adjacent hills in pursuit of unhappy partridges, wandering along the banks of the beautiful creek, whipping its tranquil surface for speckled trout, or cramming myself with grapes at the vineyard, that I have not, until this moment, found time to fulfil my promise of a continuation of my traveling adventures. I left Benicia with satisfaction. Ungrateful people! I had expected, after the very handsome manner in which I had spoken of their city; the glowing description of its magnitude, prosperity, and resources that I had given; the consequent rise in property that had taken place; the manifest effect that my letter would produce upon the action of Congress in making Benicia a port of entry; in view of all these circumstances I had, indeed, expected some trifling compliment—a public dinner, possibly, or peradventure a delicate present of a lot or two—the deeds enclosed in a neat and appropriate letter from the Town Council. But no! The name of Squibob remains unhonored and unsung, and, what is far worse, unrecorded and untaxed in magnificent Benicia. "How sharper than a serpent's thanks it is to have a toothless child," as Pope beautifully remarks in his *Paradise Lost*. One individual characterized my letter as "a d—d burlesque." I pity that person and forgive him.

For the last few days of my stay in Benicia, that city was in a perfect whirl of excitement. The election was rapidly approaching, and Herr Rossiter was exhibiting feats of legerdemain at the California House. Individuals were rushing about the streets proffering election tickets of all shapes and sizes, and tickets for the exhibition were on sale at all the principal hotels. One man conjured you to take a ticket, while another asked you to take a ticket to see the man conjured, so that, what with the wire-pulling by day, and the slack wire performance by night, you stood an excellent chance for getting slightly bewildered. Public meetings were held, where multitudes of fifty excited individuals surrounded the steps of the El Dorado, listening with breathless interest to a speech in favor of McDaniels and abusive to Bradford, or in favor of somebody else and everlastingly condemnatory of both.

Election meetings, anywhere, are always exciting and interesting spectacles, but the moral effect produced by the last which I attended in Benicia, when (after some little creature named Frisbie had made a speech, declaring his readiness to wrap himself in the Star-Spangled Banner, fire off a pistol, and die like a son of—liberty, for the Union) Dr. Simple slowly unfolded himself to his utmost height, and with one hand resting upon the chimney of the El Dorado, and the other holding his *serape* up to heaven, denounced such sentiments, and declaring that California had made him, and he should go his length for California, right or wrong, union or disunion. The moral effect, I say, produced was something more than exciting; it was sublime; it was tremendous! "That's a right-down good speech," said my fair companion, "but my! how the General gave it to him! Didn't he, Mr. Squibob?" "He did so," said I.

The candidates were all Democrats, I believe, and all but one entertained the same political sentiments. This gentleman (a candidate for the Senate), however, in the elucidation of his political principles, declared that he "went in altogether for John C. Calhoun, and nothing shorter." Now I'm no politician and have no wish to engage in a controversy on the subject; but, God forgive me if I am in error, I thought Calhoun had been dead for some months. Well, I suppose someone is elected by this time, and the waves of political excitement have become calm, but Benicia was a stormy place during the election, I assure you.

I succeeded in borrowing one dollar at ten percent a month (with security on a corner lot in Kearney Street, San Francisco), purchased a ticket, and went to see Herr Rossiter. Gracious! How he balanced tobacco pipes, and tossed knives in the air, and jumped on a wire, and sat down on it, and rolled over it, and made it swing to and fro while he threw little brass balls from one hand to the other. The applause was tremendous, and when, after a solo by the orchestra (which consisted of one seedy violin, played by an individual in such a state of hopeless inebriation that his very fiddle seemed to hiccough), he threw a back-handed summerset, and falling in a graceful attitude, informed the audience that "he should appear again tomorrow evening with a change of performance," we enthusiastically cheered, and my friend, the man in the red vest, who had sat during the whole evening in a state of rapt admiration, observed with a profound ejaculation, "that it went ahead of anything he had ever seen in his life, except the Falls of Niagara!"

I made many friends in Benicia. I don't like the place much, but I do like the people; and among my acquaintances, from Dr. Simple to my friend Mr. Sawyer—which two gentlemen may be termed the long and short of the place—I have never met with more kindness, more genuine hospitality than from the gentlemen of Benicia. The ladies are pretty, too; but to use an entirely original metaphor, which, I presume, none of your readers ever heard before or will hear again: they are "like angels' visits, few and far between." There isn't a more moral place on the face of the earth than Benicia. Ephesus, where the stupid people, a few years since, used to worship Diana, wasn't a circumstance to it.

Sonoma is twelve miles from Napa, and is—but I shall defer my description until next week, for I have scarcely made up my mind with regard to it, and my waning paper warns me I have said enough at present.

Yours for ever.

Squibob in San Francisco
October 15th, 1850

TIME! At the word Squibob comes cheerfully up to the scratch, and gracefully smiling upon his friends and supporters, lets fly his one, two, as follows:

Sonoma *is* a nice place. As my Sabbath-school instructor (peace to his memory) used to add, by way of a clincher to his dictum—Piety is the foundation of all religion—"thar can't be no doubt on't." Situated in the midst of the delightful and fertile valley which bears its name, within three miles of the beautiful creek upon whose "silvery tide, where whilom sported the tule boats of the unpleasant Indians," the magnificent [ly little] steamer *Georgina* now puffs and wheezes tri-weekly from San Francisco; enjoying an unvarying salubrious climate, neither too warm nor too cold. With little wind, few fleas, and a sky of that peculiarly blue description that Fremont terms the Italian, it may well be called, as by the sentimentally struck traveling snob it frequently is, the Garden of California.

I remained there ten whole days—somewhat of a marvel for so determined a gadabout as myself—and don't remember of ever passing ten days more pleasantly. It is useless for me to occupy time and trespass upon your patience by a lengthy description of Sonoma. If any of your readers would know the exact number of houses it contains, the names of the people who dwell therein, the botanical applications of the plants growing in its vicinity, or anything else about it that would be of any mortal use to anyone, without being positively amusing, let them purchase *Revere,* or some other equally scientific work on California, and inform themselves; suffice it to say that there is delightful society, beautiful women, brave men, and most luscious grapes to be found there; and the best thing one can possibly do, if a tired and *ennuyeed* resident of San Francisco, Benicia, or any other great city of all work and no play, is to take the *Georgina* some pleasant afternoon and go up there for a change. He'll find it!

General Smith and his staff reside at Sonoma, and a small detachment of troops have their station and quarters there. I saw a trooper in the street one day; he wore a coat with a singularly brief tail and a nose of a remarkably vivid tinge of redness. I thought he might have just returned from *the* expedition, for his limbs were evidently weakened by toil and privation, and his course along the street slow in movement and serpentine in direction. I would have asked him to proceed to the Sink of Mary's River and recover an odd boot that I left there last fall, but he looked scarcely fit to make the journey. I feared he might be Jenkins and forbore. But it's a glorious thing to reflect that we have an army at our disposal in this country, and a blessed reflection that should we lose any old clothing in the wilderness we can get Mr. Crawford to get that branch of the service to pick it up.

Tired at last of monotony, even in beautiful Sonoma, I packed up my carpet-bag, and taking the two-mule stage, passed through pretty little Napa again, and found myself, one evening, once more at Benicia. It had increased somewhat since I had left it. I observed several new clothes-poles had been erected, and noticed a handcart at the corner of a street that I had never seen before. But I had little time for observation, for the *New World* came puffing up to the hulks as I arrived, and I hastily stepped on board. Here I met my ancient crony and distinguished friend, Le Baron Vieux, who was on his way from Sacramento to the metropolis. The Baron is a good fellow and a funny man. You have frequently laughed over his drolleries in the *True Delta,* and in his usually unimpeachably "good style," he showed me about the boat, introduced me to the captain, pointed out the "model artists" who were on board, and finally capped the climax of his polite attention by requesting me to take a drink. I didn't refuse, particularly—and we descended to the bar. And "What," said the Baron with a pleasant and hospitable smile, "what, my dear fellow, will you drink?" I chose *Bine* and *Witters*—the Baron himself drinking *Bin* and *Gitters.* We hob-a-nobbed, tossed off our glasses without winking, and, for an instant, gazed at each other in gasping, unspeakable astonishment. "Turpentine and aqua fortis!" shuddered I. "Friend!" said the Baron, in an awful voice, to the barkeeper, "that drink is fifty cents; but I will with pleasure give you a dollar to tell us *what* it was we drank." "We call it," replied that imperturbable man, "Sherry Wine, but I don't know as I ever saw anyone drink it before." Quoth the Baron, who by this time had partially recovered his circulation and the consequent flow of his ideas: "I think, my friend, you'll never see it drank before or behind hereafter."

The *New World* is an excellent and, for California, an elegant boat. Her captain (who don't know Wakeman?) is a pleasant gentleman. Her accommodations are unequaled—but, and I say this expressly for the benefit of my brethren of the Dumfudgin Club, never call for

"wine and bitters" at her bar. Ascending to the cabin on the upper
deck, I had the satisfaction of a formal presentation to Dr. Collyer and
his interesting family. Sober, high-toned moral, and well-conducted
citizens may sneer if they please; rowdies may visit, and, with no other
than the prurient ideas arising from their own obscene imagination,
may endorse the same opinions more forcibly by loud ejaculations
and vulgar remarks; but I pretend to say that no right-minded man,
with anything like the commencement of a taste for the beautiful and
artistic, can attend one of these "model artist" exhibitions without
feeling astonished, gratified, and, if an enthusiast, delighted.

As our gallant boat, dashing the spray from her bow, bore us
safely and rapidly onward through the lovely bay of San Pablo, the
moon tipping with its silvery rays each curling wave around us, and
shedding a flood of yellow light upon our upper deck, "I walked with
Sappho." And "Oh, beautiful being," said I, somewhat excited by the
inspiring nature of the scene, and possibly, the least thought, by the
turpentine I had imbibed, "do you never feel, when in the pride of
your matchless charms you stand before us, the living, breathing
representation of the lovely, poetic, and ill-fated Sappho; do you
never feel an inspiration of the moment, and, entering into the
character, imagine yourself in mind, as in form, her beauteous
illustration?" "Well—yes," said she, with the slightest possible
indication of a yawn, "I don't know but I do, but it's *dreadful tearing
on the legs!*"

Hem! A steamer's motion always made me feel unpleasantly,
and the waves of San Pablo Bay ran high that evening. The Baron and
I took more turpentine immediately. We landed in your metropolis
shortly after, and succeeding in obtaining a man to carry my valise a
couple of squares, for which service, being late, he charged me but
thirty-two dollars, I repaired to and registered my name at the St.
Francis Hotel, which, being deciphered with an almost imperceptible
grin by my own and every other traveler's agreeable and gentlemanly
friend, Campbell, I received the key of number 12 and incontinently

retired to rest. What I have seen in San Francisco I reserve for another occasion. I leave for San Diego this evening, from which place I will take an early opportunity of addressing you. I regret that I cannot remain to be a participant in the coming celebration, but my cousin Skewball, a resident of the city, who writes with a keen if not a "caustic pen," has promised to furnish you an elaborate account of the affair, which, if you print, I trust you will send me.

Write me by the post orifice. *Au reservoir.*

A Struggle to Keep an Appointment

Bayard Taylor

The change from our bone-racking saddle-horses to the light, easy buggy and span of fast blacks made the commencement of our journey a veritable luxury in spite of the heat and dust. Our road led up a lateral arm of Russian River Valley, extending eastward toward the foot of Mount St. Helene. Though the country was but thinly settled, there was more than one stately two-story farmhouse standing, with a lordly air, in its natural park of oaks, and we passed—what I had been longing to see—a schoolhouse. The few cultivated fields were fenced without regard to expense—or, rather, with a proper regard to their bountiful harvests—yet the trees, whose slaughter we had lamented further down the valley, were generously spared. The oaks were hung with streamers of silver-gray

From At Home and Abroad. *New York: G.P. Putnam, 1862.*

moss, from one to three feet long, and resembling, in texture, the finest point-lace. So airy and delicate was this ornament, that the groves through which we passed had nothing of that sombre, weeping character which makes the cypress swamps of the South so melancholy. Here they were decked as if for a bridal, and slept in languid, happy beauty, in the lap of the golden hills.

More than once, the road was arbitrarily cut off, and turned from its true course, by the fencing in of new fields. This was especially disagreeable where a cove of level bottom-land had been thus enclosed, and we were forced to take the hillside, where the wheels slipped slowly along, one side being dangerously elevated above the other. I was informed (whether truly or not I cannot say) that the county has never yet located a single road—consequently, the course of the highways is wholly at the mercy of the settlers, each of whom makes whatever changes his interest or convenience may suggest. A mile of side-hill was sometimes inflicted upon us, when a difference of ten yards would have given us a level floor. Our horses, however, were evidently accustomed to these peculiarities and went on their way with a steadiness and cheerfulness which I had never seen equaled.

Still more remarkable was their intelligent manner of crossing the deep *arroyos* which we encountered near the head of the valley. There were rarely any bridges. The road plunged straight down the precipitous side of the gully, and then immediately mounted at the same angle. As we commenced the descent, the horses held back until they seemed to stand on their forefeet, poising the buggy as a juggler poises a chair on his chin. When halfway down, they cautiously yielded to the strain, sprang with a sudden impetus that took away one's breath, cleared the bottom, and, laying hold of the opposite steep as if their hoofs had been hands, scrambled to the top before the vehicle had time to recover its weight by wholly losing the impulsion. Even my inexperienced companion, to whom these descents seemed at first so perilous, was soon enabled to make them with entire confidence in the sagacity of the noble animals.

In one instance, they showed a self-possession almost human. We came to an *arroyo,* which, at first sight, appeared to be impassable. It was about forty feet deep, the sides dropping at an angle of forty-five degrees, and meeting in a pool of water at the bottom. Down we went, with a breathless rush; but, fearing that the sudden change from the line of descent to that of ascent might snap some bolt in the vehicle, I checked the speed of the horses more than was prudent. We were but halfway up the other side when the buggy recovered its weight and began to drag back. They felt, instantaneously, the impossibility of bringing it to the top; stopped; backed, with frightful swiftness, to the bottom, and a yard or two up the side they had just descended; then, leaping forward, in a sort of desperate fury, throwing themselves almost flat against the steep, every glorious muscle quivering with its tension, they whirled us to the summit. I felt my blood flush and my nerves tingle, as if I had witnessed the onset of a forlorn hope.

Finally, the valley, growing narrower, wholly lost itself in a labyrinth of low, steeply-rounded, wooded hills. The road, following the dry bed of a stream, was laboriously notched in the sides of these elevations. There was barely room for a single vehicle, and sometimes the hub of one wheel would graze the perpendicular bank, while the tire of the other rolled on the very brink of the gulf below us.

The chasms were spanned by the rudest kind of corduroy bridges. Bad and dangerous as the road was, it was really a matter of surprise that there should have been any road at all. The cost of the work must have been considerable, as the cañon is nearly two miles in length. I had every confidence in the sagacity of our horses and knew that our vehicle could safely go where a settler's cart had already gone; but there was one emergency, the possibility of which haunted me until my nerves fairly trembled. What if we should meet another vehicle in this pass! No turning out, no backing, often not even the chance of lowering one of them by ropes until the other could pass! The turnings were so sharp and frequent, that it was impossible to see any distance ahead; and I approached every corner with a temporary suspension of breath. Suddenly, in the heart of the cañon, where the bays exhaled thick fragrance in the hot air, a dust arose, and horses' heads appeared from behind a rock. My heart jumped into my mouth for an instant, then—riders, thank heaven!

"Is there a team behind you ?" I cried.

"I think not," said one of them. "Hurry on, and you're safe!"

The pass opened into a circular valley, behind which towered, in the east, the stupendous bulk of Mount St. Helene. This peak received its name from the Russian settlers, as a compliment to the Grand-Duchess Helene. It is generally called St. Helena by the Americans—who, of all people, have least sense of the fitness of names. The mountain, 5,000 feet high, rises grandly above all the neighboring chains. As seen from this point, its outline strikingly resembles that of a recumbent female figure, hidden under a pall of purple velvet. It suggests to your mind Coreggio's Magdalen and a statue of St. Cecilia in one of the churches of Rome. The head is raised and propped on the folded arms; the line of the back swells into the full, softly-rounded hip, and then sweeps away downward in the rich curve of the thigh. Only this Titaness is robed in imperial hues. The yellow mountains around are pale by contrast, and the forests of giant redwood seem but the bed of moss on which rests her purple drapery.

It was now past noon, and still a long way to Napa City, where I had engaged to lecture in the evening. I supposed, however, that we were already in Napa Valley, with all the rough and difficult part of the road behind us. Driving up to the first settler's shanty I accosted a coarse, sunburnt fellow, who was making a corral for pigs and cattle.

"How far to Napa?"

"Well (scratching his head), I don't exactly know."

"Is this Napa Valley?" I then asked.

"No," he answered, "this is Knight's Valley. You've got to pass Knight's afore you come to Napa."

Presently, another man came up with a lasso in his hand and stated, with a positive air of knowledge that was refreshing, that we had thirty miles to go. In doubtful cases, however, I never trust to a single informant; and this was the result of my inquiries in passing through Knight's Valley:

Head of valley	(to Napa City)		30 miles
A mile further	"	"	27 "
Half mile	"	"	35 "
One mile	"	"	45 "
One-fourth mile	"	"	40(!) "

After this, I gave up the attempt in despair, being satisfied that I was upon the right road and that if the place could be reached, I should reach it. At Knight's, near the eastern end of the valley, we found a company of emigrants, who had just crossed the plains and were hastening on, dusty and way-worn, to settle on Russian River. The men were greasing the wheels of their carts, while the younger children unhitched and watered the horses. The former had a sullen, unfriendly look—the result of fatigue and privation. An emigrant, at the close of such a journey, is the least social, the least agreeable of men. He is in a bad humor with the world, with life, and with his fellow men. Let him alone; in another year, when his harsh experience has been softened by memory, the latent kindness of his nature returns—unless he be an incorrigible Pike. Nothing struck me more pleasantly, during this trip, than the uniform courtesy of the people whom we met.

Crossing an almost imperceptible divide, after leaving Knight's, we found ourselves in Napa Valley. The scenery wore a general resemblance to that of Russian River, but was, if possible, still more beautiful. Mount St. Helene formed a majestic rampart on the north;

the mountain walls on either hand were higher, more picturesquely broken, and more thickly wooded; the oaks rising from the floor of the valley were heavier, more ancient—some of them, in fact, absolutely colossal—and fir trees 200 feet in height rose out of the dark glens. A wide, smooth highway, unbroken by *arroyos,* carried us onward through Druid groves, past orchards of peach and fig, farm-cottages nestled in roses, fields, and meadows, and the sunny headlands of the mountains. It was a region of ravishing beauty, and brought back, lovelier than before, the daydreams that had haunted me in the valley of San José.

As the valley grew broader and settlements became more frequent, we encountered the old plague of dust. The violet mountains, the golden fields, even the arching avenues of the evergreen oaks vanished in the black cloud, which forced me to close my eyes and blindly trust to the horses. To add to our discomfort, we were obliged to pass drove after drove of cattle, each enveloped in almost impenetrable darkness. But my gallant blacks whirled on in spite of it, and at sunset we reached a gate with the inscription "OAK KNOLL"—the welcome buoy which guided us into our harbor for the night.

Oak Knoll is the residence of Mr. Osborne, one of the largest farmers and most accomplished horticulturists in California. His ranch of 1600 acres is on the western side of the valley, four miles north of Napa City. It is a princely domain, as it comes from the hands of Nature, and its owner has sufficient taste not to meddle unnecessarily with her work. The majestic oaks she has nurtured for centuries form a splendid irregular avenue for the carriage road to his house, which stands upon the mound she placed for it, sheltered by the mountains behind, and overlooking the valley in front—no glaring mass of brick or Grecian temple with a kitchen attached, but a quaint wooden structure full of queer corners and gables, which seemed to have grown by gradual accretion. Its quiet gray tint, framed in dark green foliage, was a pleasant relief to the eye after looking on the dazzling colors of the fields and hills.

After riding to Napa City and back again to Oak Knoll in the misty night air, I felt satisfied with the day's work—twelve miles of mountain-climbing, fifty-five in a vehicle, and one lecture (equal, under the circumstances, to fifteen more!). The next evening, however, was appropriated to San Francisco involving another journey of nearly equal extent. So, with the first streak of dawn, I tore my bruised body from the delicious embrace of the bed and prepared to leave the castle. The steamer to San Francisco left Napa on alternate days, and Tuesday was not one of them. There was no other way, then, but to drive to Benicia, cross the Straits of Carquinez, take a fresh team to Oakland, and catch the last ferry boat across the Bay. It was a difficult undertaking, but it was possible. Mr. Osborne, to whom there is no such word as "fail," started us off with a cheering prediction and a basket of his choicest fruit. The five dusty miles to Napa City soon lay behind us, and I left my Petaluma team at a livery stable, in good condition.

The distance to Benicia was estimated at twenty-two miles. It was necessary that I should reach there by eleven o'clock, as the ferry boat only makes a trip every two hours. I asked for a two-horse buggy and driver, which the stablekeeper refused on the ground that there was no use for it. A less expensive team would do the business. He produced a tall, clean-limbed dun mare, which he said would "put you through." I could drive myself and leave the team in Benicia. Ten dollars. There was really no time to make any other arrangement, so I acquiesced—wondering why it is that the liverymen in California always prefer to let you drive to your destination, and then go to the trouble of sending for the team. I never obtained a driver—though I always offered to pay especially for one—without reluctance.

It was half past eight when we were fairly seated and in motion. Napa City, by daylight, resembles any young Western "city"—which means a very moderate specimen of a village. There were two or three blocks of low houses, brick and frame, ambitiously stuck against each other so as to present a metropolitan appearance—outside of these a belt of frame cottages inserted in small garden-plots, with here and there the ostentatious two-story residence of the original speculator and the "head-merchant," surmounted by a square pigeon-box, called an "observatory"—we all know how such a place looks. The population is about 800, and not likely to increase very fast, as the region supplied from this point does not extend beyond the valley. Just below the town, Napa Creek terminates in a tide water slough, which enters the Bay of San Pablo near Mare Island, forming a channel for vessels of light draught. Tule swamps, forming at first narrow belts on both sides of this slough, gradually widen as you descend the valley, until, at its mouth, they usurp nearly the whole of its surface.

It was impossible to lose the road, I was told. I therefore drove on boldly, occupied with getting the dun mare gradually warmed up to her best speed, until I noticed that we had entered a lateral valley, which lost itself in a deep cañon between two mountains to the eastward. The road was broad and well-traveled, but after proceeding two miles, it split into several branches. I began to suspect that we were on the wrong trail, and therefore hailed two women who were washing clothes near a shanty. They pointed to the main branch, which, I could see, climbed the mountain, assuring me that it was the road to Suscol—the first stage on the way to Benicia. The broad slope of the mountain was covered with a stream of lava, from an eruption thousands of years ago. The rough blocks had been cleared away from the road, but the ascent was still very toilsome. Twisted live-oaks partly shaded the highway; above us towered the mountain, bare and yellow, while the cañon, on our left, sank suddenly into a gulf of blue vapor. It was a singularly wild and picturesque spot, and I marveled that my friends had made no mention of it.

From the summit we had a prospect of great beauty. All Napa Valley, bounded to the west by the range which divides it from Sonoma, lay at our feet—the transparent golden line of the landscape changing through lilac into violet as it was swallowed up in the airy distance. The white houses of the town gleamed softly in the center of the picture. I gave our animal but a short breathing spell and hurried on, expecting to find a divide, and a valley beyond, opening south-ward toward the Straits of Carquinez. I was doomed, however, to disappointment. There was no divide; the road became very rough and irregular, with side-hill sections as it wound among the folded peaks. We passed the shanty of a settler, but nobody was at home— the tents and wagons of an emigrant party, deserted, although recently-washed shirts and petticoats hung on the bushes; and, to crown all, no one was abroad in the road. Presently, side-trails began to branch off into the glens; the main trail, which I kept, became fainter and finally—two miles further—terminated altogether in front of a lonely cabin!

A terrible misgiving seized me. To miss one's way is disagreeable under any circumstances, but to miss it when every minute is of value is one of those misfortunes which gives us a temporary disgust toward life. I sprang from the buggy, halloed, tried the doors—all in vain. "O ye generation of vipers!" I cried, "are ye never at home?" Delay was equally impracticable; so I turned the horse's head and drove rapidly back. A boy of eighteen, who came down one of the glens on horseback, thought we were on the right road but wasn't sure. At last I espied a shanty at a little distance and, leaving the buggy, hastened thither across a ploughed field, taking six furrows at a stride. A homely woman, with two upper teeth, was doing some washing under a live oak. "Which is the road to Benicia?" I gasped. "Lord bless you!" she exclaimed, "where did you come from?" I pointed to the cañon. "Sakes alive! that's jist right wrong! Why didn't you keep to the left? Now you've got to go back to Napa, leastways close on to it, and then go down the valley, follerin' the telegraph poles."

Talk of a "sinking of the heart!" My midriff gave way with a crash, and the heart fell a thousand leagues in a second. I became absolutely sick with the despairing sense of failure. Here we were, in the mountains, seven miles from Napa, all of which must be retraced.

It was a doubtful chance whether we could reach Benicia in season for the next ferry boat at 1 P.M.—and then, how were we to cross the mountains to Oakland (twenty-five miles) by 5 P.M.? It had been my boast that I *always* kept my appointments. During the previous winter I had lectured 135 times in six months without making a failure. I had ridden all night in a buggy, chartered locomotives, spent, in some instances, more than I received, but always kept the appointment. I had assured my doubting friends in San Francisco that nothing short of an earthquake should prevent me from returning in season; yet here I was, at ten o'clock in the forenoon, with sixty-six miles of mountains, bays, and straits to be overcome! The merchant who loses half his fortune by an unlucky venture is a cheerful man, if his sensations could be measured with mine.

I do not know whether other lecturers experience the same weight of responsibility. If they do, there is no more anxious and unhappy class of men. The smallest part of the disappointment, in case of failure, falls upon the lecturer himself. In the first place, the evening has been chosen by the association which engages him, with a nice regard to pecuniary success. Nothing else must interfere, to divide the attendance of the public. In the second place, 500, or 1,000, or 3,000 people, as the case may be, hurry their tea, or decline invitations, or travel many miles in order to attend; they "come early to secure good seats," wait an hour or two—the dreariest of all experiences—and then go home. It is no agreeable sensation to be responsible for the disappointment of one individual; multiply this by a thousand, and you will have the sum total of my anxiety and distress.

Back again, through the wild cañon; down the steep, whence the landscape, so sunny, before, now looked dark and wintry; over the bed of lava; across the bottom-land, and over the hill we went—until, just in the outskirts of Napa City, we found the telegraph poles and a broad road leading down the valley. Two hours and a half were still left us for the twenty-two miles. The dun mare was full of spirit, and I began to pluck up a little spirit also. Rolling along over low, treeless hills, we reached Suscol (five miles) in half an hour. The dun mare whisked her tail and stretched out her head; her hoofs beat a lively tattoo on the hard, dry soil as she trotted off mile after mile without a break. A cool wind blew up from the bay, bringing us balsam from the fields, and the ride would have been glorious if we could have enjoyed it. A carriage traveling the same way enveloped us in dust. I submitted to this, as we were approaching the town of Vallejo, opposite Mare Island, by avoiding which we could save a mile or more, and I had a presentiment that the carriage was bound for Benicia. True enough, it struck into an open trail; I followed, and in fifteen minutes found myself on the main road to Benicia. For this service I thanked the travelers by pushing ahead and giving them clouds of dust to swallow. The straits of Carquinez lay on our right, sparkling in the sun. The road crossed the feet of the bare, yellow hills, upon which the sun beat with culinary force; flecks of foam gathered on the mare's hide, but she still stepped out merrily, and at a quarter before one we were in Benicia.

The Sea Fogs

Robert Louis Stevenson

A change in the colour of the light usually called me in the morning. By a certain hour, the long, vertical chinks in our western gable, where the boards had shrunk and separated, flashed suddenly into my eyes as stripes of dazzling blue, at once so dark and splendid that I used to marvel how the qualities could be combined. At an earlier hour, the heavens in that quarter were still quietly coloured, but the shoulder of the mountain which shuts in the canyon already glowed with sunlight in a wonderful compound of gold and rose and green; and this too would kindle, although more mildly and with rainbow tints, the fissures of our crazy gable. If I were sleeping heavily, it was the bold blue that struck me awake; if more lightly, then I would come to myself in that earlier and fairier light.

From The Silverado Squatters. *London: Chatto & Windus, 1883.*

One Sunday morning, about five, the first brightness called me. I rose and turned to the east, not for my devotions, but for air. The night had been very still. The little private gale that blew every evening in our canyon, for ten minutes or perhaps a quarter of an hour, had swiftly blown itself out; in the hours that followed not a sigh of wind had shaken the treetops; and our barrack, for all its breaches, was less fresh that morning than of wont. But I had no sooner reached the window than I forgot all else in the sight that met my eyes, and I made but two bounds into my clothes, and down the crazy plank to the platform.

The sun was still concealed below the opposite hilltops, though it was shining already, not twenty feet above my head, on our own mountain slope. But the scene, beyond a few near features, was entirely changed. Napa Valley was gone; gone were all the lower slopes and woody foothills of the range; and in their place, not a thousand feet below me, rolled a great level ocean. It was as though I had gone to bed the night before, safe in a nook of inland mountains, and had awakened in a bay upon the coast. I had seen these in-undations from below; at Calistoga I had risen and gone abroad in the early morning, coughing and sneezing, under fathoms on fathoms of gray sea vapour, like a cloudy sky—a dull sight for the artist, and a painful experience for the invalid. But to sit aloft one's self in the pure air and under the unclouded dome of heaven, and thus look down on the submergence of the valley, was strangely different and even de-lightful to the eyes. Far away were hilltops like little islands. Nearer, a smoky surf beat about the foot of precipices and poured into all the coves of these rough mountains. The colour of that fog ocean was a thing never to be forgotten. For an instant, among the Hebrides and just about sundown, I have seen something like it on the sea itself. But the white was not so opaline; nor was there, what surprisingly in-creased the effect, that breathless, crystal stillness over all. Even in its gentlest moods the salt sea travails, moaning among the weeds or lisping on the sand; but that vast fog ocean lay in a trance of silence, nor did the sweet air of the morning tremble with a sound.

As I continued to sit upon the dump, I began to observe that this sea was not so level as at first sight it appeared to be. Away in the extreme south, a little hill of fog arose against the sky above the general surface, and as it had already caught the sun, it shone on the horizon like the topsails of some giant ship. There were huge waves, stationary, as it seemed, like waves in a frozen sea; and yet, as I looked again, I was not sure but they were moving after all, with a slow and august advance. And while I was yet doubting, a promontory of the hills some four or five miles away, conspicuous by a bouquet of tall pines, was in a single instant overtaken and swallowed up. It reappeared in a little, with its pines, but this time as an islet, and only to be swallowed up once more and then for good. This set me looking nearer, and I saw that in every cove along the line of mountains the fog was being piled in higher and higher, as though by some wind that was inaudible to me. I could trace its progress, one pine tree first growing hazy and then disappearing after another; although sometimes there was none of this forerunning haze, but the whole opaque white ocean gave a start and swallowed a piece of mountain at a gulp. It was to flee these poisonous fogs that I had left the seaboard, and climbed so high among the mountains. And now, behold, here came the fog to besiege me in my chosen altitudes, and yet came so beautifully that my first thought was of welcome.

The sun had now gotten much higher, and through all the gaps of the hills it cast long bars of gold across that white ocean. An eagle, or some other very great bird of the mountain, came wheeling over the nearer pine-tops, and hung, poised and something sideways, as if to look abroad on that unwonted desolation, spying, perhaps with terror, for the eyries of her comrades. Then, with a long cry, she disappeared again towards Lake County and the clearer air. At length it seemed to me as if the flood were beginning to subside. The old landmarks, by whose disappearance I had measured its advance, here a crag, there a brave pine tree, now began, in the inverse order, to make their reappearance into daylight. I judged all danger of the fog was over. This was not Noah's flood; it was but a morning spring, and would now drift out seaward whence it came. So, mightily relieved, and a good deal exhilarated by the sight, I went into the house to light the fire.

I suppose it was nearly seven when I once more mounted the platform to look abroad. The fog ocean had swelled up enormously since last I saw it; and a few hundred feet below me, in the deep gap where the Toll House stands and the road runs through into Lake County, it had already topped the slope, and was pouring over and down the other side like driving smoke. The wind had climbed along with it; and though I was still in calm air, I could see the trees tossing below me, and their long, strident sighing mounted to me where I stood.

Half an hour later, the fog had surmounted all the ridge on the opposite side of the gap, though a shoulder of the mountain still warded it out of our canyon. Napa Valley and its bounding hills were now utterly blotted out. The fog, sunny white in the sunshine, was pouring over into Lake County in a huge, ragged cataract, tossing treetops appearing and disappearing in the spray. The air struck with a little chill, and set me coughing. It smelt strong of the fog, like the smell of a washing-house, but with a shrewd tang of the sea salt.

Had it not been for two things—the sheltering spur which answered as a dyke, and the great valley on the other side which rapidly engulfed whatever mounted—our own little platform in the canyon must have been already buried a hundred feet in salt and poisonous air. As it was, the interest of the scene entirely occupied our minds. We were set just out of the wind, and but just above the fog; we could listen to the voice of the one as to music on the stage; we could plunge our eyes down into the other, as into some flowing stream from over the parapet of a bridge; thus we looked on upon a strange, impetuous, silent, shifting exhibition of the powers of nature, and saw the familiar landscape changing from moment to moment like figures in a dream.

The imagination loves to trifle with what is not. Had this been indeed the deluge, I should have felt more strongly, but the emotion would have been similar in kind. I played with the idea, as the child flees in delighted terror from the creations of his fancy. The look of the thing helped me. And when at last I began to flee up the mountain, it was indeed partly to escape from the raw air that kept me coughing, but it was also part in play.

As I ascended the mountainside, I came once more to overlook the upper surface of the fog; but it wore a different appearance from what I had beheld at daybreak. For, first, the sun now fell on it from high overhead, and its surface shone and undulated like a great nor-'land moor country, sheeted with untrodden morning snow. And next the new level must have been a thousand or fifteen hundred feet higher than the old, so that only five or six points of all the broken country below me still stood out.

Napa Valley was now one with Sonoma on the west. On the hither side, only a thin scattered fringe of bluffs was unsubmerged; and through all the gaps the fog was pouring over, like an ocean, into the clear blue sunny country on the east. There it was soon lost; for it fell instantly into the bottom of the valleys, following the watershed; and the hilltops in that quarter were still clear cut upon the eastern sky.

Through the Toll House gap and over the near ridges on the other side, the deluge was immense. A spray of thin vapour was thrown high above it, rising and falling, and blown into fantastic shapes. The speed of its course was like a mountain torrent. Here and there a few treetops were discovered and then whelmed again; and for one second, the bough of a dead pine beckoned out of the spray like the arm of a drowning man. But still the imagination was dissatisfied, still the ear waited for something more. Had this indeed been water (as it seemed so, to the eye), with what a plunge of reverberating thunder would it have rolled upon its course, disembowelling mountains and deracinating pines! And yet water it was, and seawater at that, true Pacific billows, only somewhat rarefied, rolling in midair among the hilltops.

I climbed still higher, among the red rattling gravel and dwarf underwood of Mount St. Helena, until I could look right down upon Silverado, and admire the favoured nook in which it lay. The sunny plain of fog was several hundred feet higher; behind the protecting spur a gigantic accumulation of cottony vapour threatened with every second, to blow over and submerge our homestead; but the vortex setting past the Toll House was too strong; and there lay our little platform, in the arms of the deluge, but still enjoying its unbroken sunshine. About eleven, however, thin spray came flying over the friendly buttress, and I began to think the fog had hunted out its Jonah after all. But it was the last effort. The wind veered while we were at dinner, and began to blow squally from the mountain summit, and by half-past one, all that world of sea fogs was utterly routed and flying here and there into the south in little rags of cloud. And instead of a lone sea-beach, we found ourselves once more inhabiting a high mountainside with the clear green country far below us, and the light smoke of Calistoga blowing in the air.

This was the great Russian campaign for that season. Now and then, in the early morning, a little white lakelet of fog would be seen far down in Napa Valley; but the heights were not again assailed, nor was the surrounding world again shut off from Silverado.

from Vines in the Sun

Idwal Jones

The day was beautiful and without haze. After the early mist from the San Joaquin has lifted, the air is so clear that the houses seem like freshly painted Noah's Arks, and the fields as dustless and sharply colored as a rinsed palette. An infinity of small vineyards was about us. The trees are high and umbrageous; the hillocky slopes, tufted with live-oaks, each in its dark pool of shadow, seem ready to flow down into your lap, for the landscape has become miniature, half English. There are even sheep, and poked through a fence you may see rams' heads, for the tarweed in the ditches is greener than the grass in the fields.

It was mid-August, the vines and the road thick under dust, and the sun lay athwart our necks like a flaming sword. But even in full summer, Napa Valley, the region of the grape, and Mount St. Helena, the purple, rounded dome at the far end, shadowing the geysers, is one of the pleasantest sights in all California. On the hillsides and by the road, the old wineries, built of hewn stone, mantled with ivy, remind you of woodcuts in *The Pilgrims of the Rhine*.

Then and there we projected a book about vineyards. The painter was to draw the pictures, and I was to put down the words.

"How will it begin?" he asked. "You won't have a lot of dates, I hope, and too much talk of the sandaled padres, and the missions, and history. I read only for pleasure."

"Then we shall begin in the middle, if I can find a middle. And I shall diffuse pleasure by not giving any dates, except when a date really must be put down. And we can't ignore the padres any more than we could ignore the Pilgrims if we were to write about Plymouth Rock. They planted the vine, and behind them trod civilization—the logical *sequitur*. There is no culture without the wine cellar and the carafe.

"I don't think their Mission grape is much esteemed now. Assuredly not for such a grape did the centaurs fight, nor for its fermented juice did Virgil sing. It was mediocre but useful, and the Franciscans wrought their honest best with it. Especially did the Señor Padre Duran of San Jose, who made a twice-distilled brandy from its wine. It was a bulwark against the onslaught of the harsh sea fogs, and as strong, they say, 'as the reverend father's faith.' Do you know how many vineyards there are in California? Twenty thousand. I suppose to be really thorough we should visit them all."

"In this heat? I should say not! We are not working for the Department of Agriculture. Twenty would be enough."

"Or ten," I rejoined. "There's one up the side road now. The old Frett place."

It was a ten-minute climb by motorcar. The house built by Jean Frett was ruinous, and the cooperage in the cave in the hillside had fallen into kindling-wood. I had camped in the house once while on a tour through the valley, after driving out a family of coyotes. This was a small grape farm, lost in a manzanita wood odorous with wild lilac, and watered at the edge by a tumbling brook.

Frett was from Alsace, a taciturn, sun-blackened farmer with learning in chemistry. He made vermouths at the valley winery, and he blended wines like "Hermitage," which requires not only the black Sirah grape but the white Roussanne and three others now vanished from these farms. With his earnings he bought three new acres to clear, to break and put under Roussannes. Then trouble befell this Eden. Prohibition came; the air was dense with smoke from burning vines, and Frett stayed on, whistling vacantly, a bankrupt like half his neighbors, then left on foot and was seen no more. *De minimis non curat lex.* The law is not concerned with trifles. A new proprietor grafted the vineyard over to Alicante, a coarse and prodigal yielder, and it was flourishing on its own, with none to guard it but the coyotes and the whirring rattlesnake.

While my companion the artist sketched over by the fence, I looked about in the old winery at the cave. It was hung all over with almanacs and posters in color, to which time had given a coffee-tinted gloss. Someone long before Frett had amassed these, and had also pasted upon the door a handful of labels. Some archaeologist a century hence, so I fancied, might up this door and, like the discoverer of the Rosetta Stone, regard himself as fortune's dearest child. Much history of the valley could be read on these stickers; I wrote down a few names, like Oak Grove, Mrs. Snowball, and Dr. Hiram Beers, names which could now stir the memories only of elders in St. Helena. In those remoter days it was the custom for nearly every small grower to affix to his bottles his own label. Good Mrs. Snowball, perchance, may have won a prize at the County Fair with her Claret, and the following Christmas, after it had aged in the bottle one more year, made gifts of it to her friends and the needy. So with Dr. Beers, the Episcopal rector, as learned in the grape as in the gospel, who was one of the first to grow hereabouts that vine of the Chianti, the San Gioveto, whose juice requires no blending nor any correction. It was an example that no one followed. His favorite jest, a reply to those hardy enough to quote him the admonishment not to look upon the wine when it is red, was, "No, a man should wait until it is older and tawny."

The custom of labeling one's own vintage has declined, and today valley labels are few. Seventy or more years ago at least five large and generous wines of the burgundy type, made in small parcels, carried far the name of this valley, of which none has written better than Robert Louis Stevenson, who came here to spend his honeymoon on the slope of Mount St. Helena.

"Wine in California," he wrote then, "is still in the experimental stage....The beginning of vine-planting is like the beginning of mining for precious metals: the winegrower also 'prospects.' One corner of land after another is tried with one kind of grape after another. This is a failure; that is better; a third best. So, bit by bit, they grope about for their Clos Vougeot and Lafite. These lodes and pockets of earth, more precious than the precious ores, that yield inimitable fragrance and soft fire; those virtuous Bonanzas, where the soil has sublimated under the sun and stars to something finer, and the wine is bottled poetry: these still lie undiscovered; chaparral conceals, thicket embowers them; the miner chips the rock and wanders farther, and the grizzly muses undisturbed. But there they bide their hour, awaiting their Columbus; and nature nurses and prepares them. The smack of Californian earth shall linger on the palate of your grandson."

It was in 1880 when he wrote of the "blood and sun in that old flask behind the faggots" on these rough hillside farms: a dolorous era of trade when the planter was living from hand to mouth, though the vine itself in novel varieties was prosperous, and multiplying on the foothills in leagues of green. Krug was flourishing then and grew a near cousin to the Margaux; the legendary Finn, Captain Niebaum, at his gothic winery was growing a Claret which, bottled in that year, was tasted at a dinner in San Francisco three years ago, and though overtaken somewhat by age, was yet a sound and honorable Claret. Bonanzas had been found up in the green and tangled thickets; tracts of stony earth hot in the long, dry summers were planted to vines chary of yield but opulent in quality, and the names of their guardians were long uttered with praise in the valley. They are still so uttered, and you know that a mythos, a tradition, exists, that is still valid and heartening—even if measured in decades and not by millennia as in legend-encrusted Europe, of which this valley is an outpost. That countryside withers that has not its lore, its arcana, and those that serve the tutelary genius of its earth, which hereabouts was Dionysus, enamored of these sunny hillsides where the bees lob drowsily in the thyme-scented air and the spade chunks hardly into the gravelly, red-dusty soil.

The first two years of the 1880s were portentous in this valley. The Oriental Exclusion Act was passed, and the small-handed workmen in pigtails trooped from the vineyards that for thirty years had known their ministering. A few stayed on, devoted to their vines, and fearful of what might happen to their charges—which was evil fortune enough, for the horse marines and city recruits brought in bungled through them lamentably with plow and hoe. It was an evil that righted itself in time, so far as it concerned the plants and not the life in the valley.

I fell into talk with a grower near Calistoga one evening at the hotel, and he threw his memory back to recall that event. "I was very small then, and we were living just this side of St. Helena. It was a dark night, and I stood by the gate of our farm, watching them go by, on foot, on horseback, some riding in laden wagons, others pushing handcarts; and the parade was lighted by lanterns at the end of poles. My father was one of the vineyardists that lent a wagon, for our Wah Lee had worked for us nearly thirty years.

"They weren't the Mongolian Peril to us. They were old Wah Lee with his pigtail who rode me on his shoulders while he bossed the grape pickers. He did the cooking, ran the vegetable garden, and made kites with long tails that went up into the sky and stayed up there as if spiked. Every farm had its Wah Lee, and as good a one as it deserved. We were all sad at their going. But Dennis Kearney, the sand-lots orator, and his crowd had then everything to say. Napa Valley folk were helpless, as helpless as they were forty years later when half of them were ruined by the 'noble experiment.'"

As workmen these Chinese, who had all been bred to gardening, were careful of all living things, and of such small and delicate fruit as apricots, figs, and grapes. Often they finished their harvesting in moonlight, moving about as silently as ghosts. The mark of their labor is to be seen everywhere in the valley from Yountville to Calistoga where the road begins to wind up the great wooded ramp of Mount St. Helena. In the seasonal lulls when the vines had grown and the sun was ripening the grapes, the valley rang with clangor as these workmen plied their chisels, cutting tunnel-like caves into the hillsides. The rock is soapstone; it cuts fairly easily when first exposed, and fast hardens. The slopes are honeycombed, and behind any clump of manzanita or sycamore on the hillside may be the hidden entrance to a maze where wine sleeps in a rock-bound world whose temperature in wet December or smoldering August is almost constant at sixty-two degrees. Then there is the visible handicraft in the stone fronts of the roadside warehouses, now covered with ivy: the megalithic Greystone winery, that other at Calistoga patterned after the Château Lafite, and four or five more, whose design have a look of ethical substance, solid and magisterial, as hard as their granite and limestone. They and the vines give an antique air to this country so young that the first Americans appeared in it long after Victoria was born.

I never knew a Chinese who was in the proper sense a vineyardist. The palate of that race in fluids stronger than tea favors distillation of apricots rather than the blood of the grape, and quite as often that rice spirit, *ng-ka-py,* which comes in squat, thin-necked bottles with a flaring lip, and to my taste, though I respect its fire, something like a brew of doormats.

But I came upon the track of a Chinese of another sort. This was up around Glen Ellen, where lived many Portuguese. They had built a new church and given an artist whom I knew an order to paint a mural of St. Mark of Lisbon. It was Caesar or nothing with these Portuguese; their St. Mark had to be twelve feet high, not an inch less. This was awkward for the painter, for his workshop in San Francisco was hardly more than a cell. By luck he found near Glen Ellen an empty, two-story edifice that for ages had been a Chinese laundry. The ground floor was eight feet high. If the ceiling were cut in two, and one end of it dropped, then the downstairs part would be tall enough to house that mural. The space would be railed off, with a balcony effect, and huge paper lanterns could dangle into the shadowy profundity from the rafters. This and other details were poured into the ear of the Portuguese owner, who was the village shoemaker. Instead of being outraged, or stunned, he was first doubt-ful, then enchanted. Nothing was too good for San Marcos, a great saint indeed! And when the masterpiece was done, then a festival would be held here, and an unveiling, with a band, plenty of wine, and the Bishop himself in attendance. He brought in tools, and the two of us and the landlord set to work upstairs, cutting into the floor along the walls.

Tribulation was lying in wait for us. The augers went so far and no farther, the chisels jounced up, and the first saw that screeched through came up sans teeth, and so did the next. As well try to saw a battleship in two as that ceiling, which was covered with a layer of flattened-out tin. Bow Sang Kee had armored it against the steam rising from the wash tubs below, being not only thorough in his craft, but also a model tenant. So there was nothing for it but to perch on step-ladders, and use up a gross of can-openers, ripping through an acre of tin for the glory of San Marcos of Lisbon.

No one could survive that ordeal and not be curious over Bow Sang Kee, and still less after seeing in his woodshed a large stack of bottles, "dead men" of labeled eminence. There were even flasks that had held the amber sunshine of Johannisberger from Metternich's vineyard, and such prodigies as Rauzan-Ségla and Clos Vougeot. Most of them were from estates in Sonoma, and bearing names lost since Prohibition. Bow Sang Kee was one of the Chinese that had trooped out with the rest, but he had returned and set himself up in business as a washerman. He had long worked in the neighborhood as a pruner and handyman about the vats—at Dunfillan, a remarkable vineyard planted to vines from Château Margaux, and at Ten Oaks, owned by Mrs. Kate Warfield, a redoubtable lady whose cakes and crochet-work won prizes at the State Fair, whose Claret won gold medals in Germany, and who distilled all the brandy drunk in the neighborhood. Bow Sang Kee had also acquired the knack of tasting, and was known to the local vintners as a "matcher." He sampled the musts, or fermented juice in the vats, before and after blending, and judged how far it fell short of the wine that was aimed at. The vintners—and surely, if they aimed at Rauzan-Ségla, they felt they were copying the sunset—must have watched Bow Sang Kee anxiously as he swirled the glass and clucked his tongue. Bow Sang Kee got much wine in recompense for his judging, and now and then bought costly, imported marks to correct his palate.

He was an amateur, to use a good word dulled by misuse, a lover of wine for its own sake, and for the rest a good laundryman whose gloss with the iron was well spoken of. Good wine needed no bush as sign to him, nor label, for though he understood winery talk in English, French, and German, he read them no more than he read Etruscan. The pomp and glory of Rozlan, Johannisberger with its innocence and sprightly grace, the seal on these evoked for him no rush of old and poetic associations. They were something to taste and drink; and with no help of tradition he appraised them on their own virtues. He had an unprejudiced palate, a high set of values, and candor. Sir Osbert Sitwell would call these the tests of a civilized man. One can see our Chinaman, after a hard day at the washboard, sitting under his fig tree with bamboo pipe, bottle, and taster's glass, a bubble shaped like a decapitated egg. He swirls his glass, taking in the color, the aroma, the slow falling-back of the "tears of the wine," with a smile of anticipation. For that glass of Hippocrene an emperor would envy him; but Bow Sang Kee could have envied no man.

We shall consider a certain gathering of eight men about a table at Platt's Hall in San Francisco. It was April 1880. The winegrowing industry, after a hundred years, had fallen into dolorous plight. Phylloxera, the same "unconquerable worm" that had laid waste all of Burgundy and the Rhone country, was on the rampage, and had destroyed a hundred of the large vineyards of California. The breath of another malady had withered the German colony at Anaheim in the south, and that plague was creeping up the coast. There had also been over-planting. Speculators, adventurers, gentlemen of much leisure and wealth, these had put vast acreages under grapevines. The price of wine had fallen so low that many farmers had abandoned their holdings.

A pint's a pound the world around, and the railroad tariff of twelve cents a pound was high; for wine it was exorbitant. Wine could be sent by boat to England, where it should have been in demand after the disaster to the vineyards on the Continent. Some threescore growers in California had achieved quality. The hocks of Jacob Schram were drunk at the Carlton Club in London; the red wines of Isaac De Turk were known in the old restaurants of Copenhagen and Danzig. At Sonoma growers like the Dresels, Jacob Gundlach, and Charles Bundschu—their names still echo after the dark night of Prohibition even if their wines are no more—were men of taste and learning, who in a leisurely age made wine in small parcels on their hillside farms, and had as much skill as any cellar-master along the Rhine.

But organization was loose; of the true guild spirit there was none. In the main, growers were still groping; each farmer had to learn for himself by trial and error what breed of grape in conjunction with the soil and climate would flourish best on this upland or that slope. Was an hour or two of sunshine after morning fog as propitious as half a day of shade and a soft basking in the sun before dusk fell? The dichotomy of north and south is political, not climatic, in California, where the great interior valley meanders up a thousand miles, as far as from Sicily to the upper Rhine, with a Moroccan sun overhead all summer; and to find coolness for his vines a man shifts westward, towards the sea. Yet even in the center of California are pockets with variations of heart and incidences of mist, but always the isothermic belts run straight up and down, not wavily across. Every acre of Europe is on the charts; the peculiarity of the acre's soil has been known since the Middle Ages. California may not be exhaustively prospected by the viticulturists for two or three more centuries; it took as long as that for Spain to find its lone sherry region, and longer for France to find its Romanée-Conti.

California after a century had not yet had its real start. And there was the affair of the *Stella*. Loaded down with wines less than good, the *Stella* had been despatched by a syndicate to the European market that was clamorous after the ruin of the vineyards. Her wines were no more evil than the sham fluids of Hamburg, with its "Hambro sherry" made of potato spirit and flavorings; nor worse than those of Cette where chemists on the docks sophisticated "Claret" from Algeria to resemble, at least to the eye, a half dozen other varieties of wine. They are gone now, those dock manufactories, done away with by law, but Cette had been in that trade since the time of Caesar, and it had the sanction of antique custom. The *Stella* had come too late in history; and monopoly was affronted. Her cargo was no such hell's broth, but the uproar over it echoed to the heavens.

The affair of the *Stella* was still rankling California when those eight men gathered to consider what had to be done. They formed a Viticultural Commission, the first effective group of the sort the state ever had. The eight who set themselves to the task of reform and of codification of wine laws were in character, it is generally agreed, the most striking group to assemble since that first Vigilance Committee which pulled order out of chaos after the Gold Rush. Each was eminent in the winegrowing trade of his own region (and the regions were seven); and his probity was unassailable. The most remarkable was Charles A. Wetmore, a Commissioner at large and the Secretary besides, who formed the group and brought it into power as a legal force. He was a staff writer on the old *Alta California*, the paper on which Mark Twain had been a reporter. Sent to Europe to report on the vineyards, Wetmore wrote home a series of thirty-four papers that had a stirring effect on the growers. He wrote also a treatise on grape varieties, an ampelography still of worth.

"Wetmore," said Frona Eunice Wait, who wrote on wine history for Bancroft, the publisher, "has a striking physical and mental resemblance to General Ben Butler."

Unlike that General, the favorite of President Grant, this journalist lost no battles. He won them; he made reforms, had bills passed that were the first of the Pure Food laws, and hammered at his notion until it became the general knowledge that California was not one country but seven, that Cucamonga in the south had the climate of Tunis, that Napa and Livermore valleys were like Bordeaux, that Guerneville, where vines grew about redwood stumps, was like the Rhine without Jack Frost.

Wetmore's jaw was iron-bound, his will resolute.

"Do we go straight ahead from here, gentlemen?" he asked, glancing about the table.

The seven lacked no more in resolution than he, and they nodded at the Chairman. Some of them were pioneers, who had begun their plowing when the bear and the Indian were still in the field. They were men of affairs, but business for them was no game of beggar-my-neighbor. They were in the business of winegrowing, which is half a science and half an art, and were ready to be out of pocket to start things going. Their experience they pooled at once, to make it available to the smallest grower, and the University of

California helped. A chair of viticulture was set up, and soon it was filled by young Professor Bioletti, who became even more renowned than the Dean of Agriculture, Eugene W. Hilgard, and the botanist, Professor George Husmann.

The phylloxera pest was largely overcome. The old vines were torn up, roots of the native American variety of grapes, resistant to the pest, were planted, and upon them were grafted cuttings of the finest European stock. Husmann was still a champion of the Norton, a red wine grape that flourishes best in Virginia; but this was a new age, and California was known to be another Europe. Wetmore himself, certain that the vineyards should start again from scratch, brought in shiploads of cuttings from Bordeaux. The standards for wine were raised. Vineyards became a staple of talk, and forty millions were suddenly invested in them. There was faith in Wetmore, in the Commissioners, and in their President, Arpad Haraszthy, son of the legendary Colonel Agoston Haraszthy, regarded as the father of viti- culture in the state. Later, Charles A. Wetmore was to be President, but the heavy work was now done; and there had been achieved a method, which as Professor Whitehead has remarked, is an invention, often greater than the sum of its details.

For the time being, California was the world's laboratory for vinegrowing, and France replanted her own vineyards to root-stock of the green grape, Noah, first grown by a German farmer in Illinois eighty years ago. The phylloxera likes not the thick integument of its roots. In California the Rupestris St. George is the root-stock for heavy-yielding plants on the valley floors in the north. Where the soil is wet, a hybrid root like Mourvedre x Rupestris 1202 is favored. For shy-bearing grapes there are other root-stocks; but on the shallow and dry hillside the cuttings had best grow their own roots. The list of root-stocks, for this region and that, for wine and table grapes, and for raisins, runs into the thousands; no man has them catalogued in his head, and their propagation is a recondite science. The problem of combating the nematode, or root borer, one of the trickiest of pests, may be solved in some tomorrow, but the farmer has to pull up his blighted Malagas and Ribiers, those fancy table grapes, and replace them with the Thompson Seedless, that grape which was born to be a raisin.

In viticulture many things are still past finding out. You dip into monographs of Dr. Maynard Amerine or Joseph Perelli-Minetti to see why the Eastern table grapes like the Concord, the Catawba, the Vergennes, flourish less well in California than they do on the eastern seaboard, where their "foxy" aroma takes you full in the nose, and though you may learn many things you will not learn that. They grow, these natives, only in the gardens of transplanted New Englanders, who bite into their Catawbas and are instantly home again in their ancestral grape bower. The Californian prefers to grow the Olivette Blanche for his table, or the odd and long Rish Baba, heat-lovers both. Once, long ago, I knew an old Frenchman high up in the Sierra foothills, at Columbia, who had an arbor full of Black Prince grapes, and remembered Mark Twain who was then tarrying at nearby Jackass Hill, and not doing anything much except tinkering on the story of *The Jumping Frog*. His grapes were inky-black, ellipsoid rather than spherical, sweet as Greek honey, long as your thumb, and exceedingly crisp. Nowhere else grew the pampered Black Prince half so sweet and large; and in the autumn he had the resource of a pear-tree, the Admiral Gervais whose fruits blacken almost at a touch and must be nursed in straw. A nephew of his fell heir to this place on the ramp of the Sierra and, for the sake of the grapes and the pears, moved into it, to the envy of all the gardeners on this oak-shaded flat.

Uncomely and poor to the eye are the true wine grapes. The white Riesling and the Sauvignon Blanc, the austere Pinots, of which some are collectors' pieces, are among the aristocrats, but are ill-formed in clusters, thin and withered, shy-bearing. They ask no more than to cling to some dry, unpropitious hillside, and be left alone.

Their yield is a sixth of the lusty commoners like the Alicante who prefer the valley floor; scarcely more than a ton to the acre, but their admirers even love them for their parsimony.

Wetmore was one of these. Now that the Viticultural Commission was a going concern, he rode about in the back country, and at the edge of Livermore Valley, where glens, firs, and scrub-oak abound as it edges towards Pleasanton. Above a rolling of hillocks stands a limestone face, the half of a dome bisected in an avalanche, and this estate, dominated by the white face, Cresta Blanca, has in wet months an air as Scottish as the Trossachs. It was given over to sheep when Wetmore bought it and fenced it in. Here he set up as wine-grower on his own account, planting the hillsides to vines he had chosen on a horseback tour of the Médoc and Sauternes regions in France, and at the Paris Exposition ten years later he was awarded gold medals for two of the wines picked at random from the bins in the long, cool tunnel driven under the hill that was the namesake for his estate.

Cresta Blanca, skirting the *arroyo,* its hills crowned with oaks, nutmeg, and sweet bay, as much home as farm, was ever one of the most beautiful of vineyards, and the prototype of many such estates in Napa Valley. Its wines, beginning with the Graves and Sauternes types, grown on shallow, pebbly loam, were beyond reproach, and report of them cast an aura over the Livermore region. There its owner during another spell of years when the trade was living from hand to mouth, with wines down to fifteen cents a gallon, sold his wine only in the bottle, and profited well by his vintages and his foresight.

Wetmore was followed by his brother Clarence, a wine technician who had been a disciple of Husmann. Charles's son, Louis, had talent of another order; he was naturally a manager, in business imaginative, and he cared for no tight check-rein. It was the custom of the trade for vintners to apprentice their sons elsewhere, and at fourteen Louis was sent to learn the craft under George West, a pioneer and a member of that first Viticultural Commission. West's holdings by a merger, became twice as large, and eight years later Louis was their head, active in running seven wineries in the hot Fresno region, of which El Pinal, with redwood tanks holding four million gallons, was the largest. The firm had its storage and bottling cellars in San Francisco. The earthquake of 1906 and the dynamiting to stop the flames wrecked most of the trade's cellars in that district. Word of that ruin was enough for Louis, who happened to be in the vineyards, and tearing along the San Joaquin in a buggy, he chartered a river steamer here, a pair of barges there, and three days later his flotilla tied up at the edge of a city still lost under smoke. The cellars were a shambles of bashed vats, barrels, and bottles, the wood floating in a red medium eight feet deep. This Admiral of twenty-four and his crew, workmen brought in from the farms, laid pipe lines, and after securing a number of fire engines—how he got them is a mystery—he pumped out the cellars, siphoning the wine into the holds of his string of barges which were hauled by twos and threes up the river, and moving it into his wineries to be distilled. Some millions of gallons of wine were salvaged and turned into brandy.

After the rebuilding he established a line of wine tank cars, which still exists as the California Despatch Line, and that done, he embarked on a far grander venture. This was to build tank steamers to carry wine to the ports of the world, to sell it to the laboring classes from England and Scotland to Australia, more cheaply even than France bought her flood of Algerian wine; indeed, Louis would sell it cheaper than milk. Quantity and excellence go rarely in hand, least of all in wine. It was bulk trade that engrossed Louis, the shifting of large amounts of cheap but sound wine to regions where spirits were heavily drunk. The notion made quite a stir in the London press, which regarded it with favor. Claret at sixpence the bottle would do wonders in the dietary of a citizenry partial to gin, and to whelks and tinned salmon, washed down with thin tea.

On the whole, the plan seemed feasible. Louis was the most powerful figure in the trade of the Fresno district, which includes the seven southern counties of the great Central or San Joaquin Valley, an empire unto itself, and so wide that most of its vineyards are out of sight of the mountains to the east and the west. For eight of the growing months in the year the sunshine is continuous, warm, and often intense. The water supply is inexhaustible, irrigation is everywhere the custom. This is the raisin empire, and it has not the austerity, the rigor, to produce dry wines of merit, save a little from grapes grown on its distant hillsides. Its yield is of barbaric opulence, and it is famous for raisins made of the Muscatel de Gordo Blanco, or the Muscat of Alexandria, which makes a table wine having, like that from the Mission, the Alicante, and the Grenache, which here flourish by its side, little or no character.

"The soil seems to impart to the vine a vigor unknown elsewhere in the world," wrote the rhapsodic Mrs. Wait years ago. "Life springs up eternal, and the perpetual sunshine allows it to thrive and grow and spread unhindered...the branches spread out in a way that is amazing; and the new life, untouched by frost or snow or ice or dew, causes new blossoms to start ere the first crop is gathered. The second crop is often nearly equal to the first, and the third crop comes before the leaves, from force of habit, drop off."

This is hyperbole, for what she mistook for the second and the third crops were but gleanings of fruit unripe at the time of the first picking. There is but one crop a year, but that one crop is a weighty eruption of grapes. This, then, was the reservoir that Louis was to tap to slake the world's thirst; this plain of enormous vineyards; of Armenian millionaires, of thirty separate towns, of crushing plants and concrete and redwood vats of an immensity peculiar to the region. The outbreak of war in 1914 held up his plans; he changed over from steel to wooden vessels, then fate played the trump card of Prohibition, and that was the end of the scheme. The last of the Cresta Blanca family, and the most spectacular, though his name seldom appeared in print, then turned to the raising of cattle and wheat.

This inland empire suffered little in the arid decade. Great and profitable was the Muscat of Alexandria that yielded raisins, even more lushly profitable was the black and bountiful Alicante, a grape of low merit, but attractive to the eye, and of a tough hide that enabled it to withstand perfectly the cross-country journey in the era when Claret was contraband and its grapes priceless.

It was the table wine regions that suffered most, the countless "pocket farms" in the Napa and Livermore valleys, the cooler and shaded slopes in five northern counties. Some of the older Catholic growers made a little altar wine and were thankful to keep alive the family craft and their vineyards. Other farms sprouted on their fine Médoc roots the coarse grafts of Alicante, Mataro, Aspiran Noir—known to the simpler as "Aspirins"—and that burly, gross-yielder, Pagadebito, "the debt-payer," crushed only for "red ink."

And there was Frett, who grew Roussanne in his once perfect small vineyard that we had come to this morning. He would no more have grafted those rough growths on his root-stocks than he would have put his arm into a fire. The night of blunder and confusion would be long; he said good-bye to his hillside and left the vines to the gopher and dove.

My companion appeared with a sketch.

"I couldn't do a better picture than this. Not in this heat. The paint dries too fast. Is it any cooler in Calistoga?"

We looked at our regional charts. They have not the detail of the wonderful maps the French have of their grape districts, with every farm down in a different color, every hedge marked. But these California charts are in their way quite as extraordinary. They are based on the work of Professor Bioletti who marked out five major climatic zones. Winkler and Amcrine have further divided them into sub-regions—all varying in rainfall, wind, and "degree days" of sunshine.

The factors are not constant. A Himalaya of fog or a spell of prolonged and burning heat may visit any zone, and if the influence is favorable, it will be a "vintage year," for in California the coolest regions grow their best wine in their hot years, warmest regions in their relatively cool years.

Calistoga is only eight miles down the road, but it is in isothermic Region Three (St. Helena being in Region Two) and akin, on the charts, to San Luis Obispo, four hundred miles to the south.

"Five degrees warmer?" said the artist. "You make a start. I'll catch up with you in the autumn."

He did not catch up with me until after five autumns, having a long engagement in France, where he saw more of battles than vintages.

The Death of Halpin Frayser

Ambrose Bierce

I

For by death is wrought greater change than hath been shown. Whereas in general the spirit that removed cometh back upon occasion, and is sometimes seen of those in flesh (appearing in the form of the body it bore) yet it hath happened that the veritable body without the spirit hath walked. And it is attested of those encountering who have lived to speak thereon that a lich so raised up hath no natural affection, nor remembrance thereof, but only hate. Also, it is known that some spirits which in life were benign become by death evil altogether.—Hali

One dark night in midsummer a man waking from a dreamless sleep in a forest lifted his head from the earth, and staring a few moments into

From Can Such Things Be? *New York: Albert & Charles Boni, 1924.*

the blackness, said: "Catherine Larue." He said nothing more; no reason was known to him why he should have said so much.

The man was Halpin Frayser. He lived in St. Helena, but where he lives now is uncertain, for he is dead. One who practices sleeping in the woods with nothing under him but the dry leaves and the damp earth, and nothing over him but the branches from which the leaves have fallen and the sky from which the earth has fallen, cannot hope for great longevity, and Frayser had already attained the age of thirty-two. There are persons in this world, millions of persons, and far and away the best persons, who regard that as a very advanced age. They are the children. To those who view the voyage of life from the port of departure the bark that has accomplished any considerable distance appears already in close approach to the farther shore. However, it is not certain that Halpin Frayser came to his death by exposure.

He had been all day in the hills west of the Napa Valley, looking for doves and such small game as was in season. Late in the afternoon it had come on to be cloudy, and he had lost his bearings; and although he had only to go always downhill—everywhere the way to safety when one is lost—the absence of trails had so impeded him that he was overtaken by night while still in the forest. Unable in the darkness to penetrate the thickets of manzanita and other undergrowth, utterly bewildered and overcome with fatigue, he had lain down near the root of a large madroño and fallen into a dreamless sleep. It was hours later, in the very middle of the night, that one of God's mysterious messengers, gliding ahead of the incalculable host of his companions sweeping westward with the dawn line, pronounced the awakening word in the ear of the sleeper, who sat upright and spoke, he knew not why, a name, he knew not whose.

Halpin Frayser was not much of a philosopher, nor a scientist. The circumstance that, waking from a deep sleep at night in the midst of a forest, he had spoken aloud a name that he had not in memory and hardly had in mind did not arouse an enlightened curiosity to investigate the phenomenon. He thought it odd, and with a little perfunctory shiver, as if in deference to a seasonal presumption that the night was chilly, he lay down again and went to sleep. But his sleep was no longer dreamless.

He thought he was walking along a dusty road that showed white in the gathering darkness of a summer night. Whence and whither it led, and why he traveled it, he did not know, though all seemed simple and natural, as is the way in dreams; for in the Land Beyond the Bed, surprises cease from troubling, and the judgment is at rest. Soon he came to a parting of the ways; leading from the highway was a road less traveled, having the appearance, indeed, of having been long abandoned, because, he thought, it led to something evil; yet he turned into it without hesitation, impelled by some imperious necessity.

As he pressed forward he became conscious that his way was haunted by invisible existences whom he could not definitely figure to his mind. From among the trees on either side he caught broken and incoherent whispers in a strange tongue which yet he partly understood. They seemed to him fragmentary utterances of a monstrous conspiracy against his body and soul.

It was now long after nightfall, yet the interminable forest through which he journeyed was lit with a wan glimmer having no point of diffusion, for in its mysterious lumination, nothing cast a shadow. A shallow pool in the guttered depression of an old wheel rut, as from a recent rain, met his eye with a crimson gleam. He stooped and plunged his hand into it. It stained his fingers; it was blood! Blood, he then observed, was about him everywhere. The weeds growing rankly by the roadside showed it in blots and splashes on their big, broad leaves. Patches of dry dust between the wheelways were pitted and spattered as with a red rain. Defiling the trunks of the trees were broad maculations of crimson, and blood dripped like dew from their foliage.

All this he observed with a terror which seemed not incompatible with the fulfillment of a natural expectation. It seemed to him that it was all in expiation of some crime which, though conscious of his guilt, he could not rightly remember. To the menaces and mysteries of his surroundings, the consciousness was an added horror. Vainly he sought, by tracing life backward in memory, to reproduce the moment of his sin; scenes and incidents came crowding tumultuously into his mind, one picture effacing another, or commingling with it in confusion and obscurity, but nowhere could he catch a glimpse of what he sought. The failure augmented his terror; he felt as one who has murdered in the dark, not knowing whom nor why. So frightful was the situation—the mysterious light burned with so silent and awful a menace; the noxious plants, the trees that by common consent are invested with a melancholy or baleful character, so openly in his sight conspired against his peace; from overhead and all about came so audible and startling whispers and the sighs of creatures so obviously not of earth that he could endure it no longer, and with a great effort to break some malign spell that bound his faculties to silence and inaction, he shouted with the full strength of his lungs! His voice broken, it seemed, into an infinite multitude of unfamiliar sounds, went babbling and stammering away into the distant reaches of the forest, died into silence, and all was as before. But he had made a beginning at resistance and was encouraged. He said:

"I will not submit unheard. There may be powers that are not malignant traveling this accursed road. I shall leave them a record and an appeal. I shall relate my wrongs, the persecutions that I endure—I, a helpless mortal, a penitent, an unoffending poet!" Halpin Frayser was a poet only as he was a penitent: in his dream.

Taking from his clothing a small red-leather pocketbook, one-half of which was leaved for memoranda, he discovered that he was without a pencil. He broke a twig from a bush, dipped it into a pool of blood, and wrote rapidly. He had hardly touched the paper with the point of his twig when a low, wild peal of laughter broke out at a measureless distance away, and growing ever louder, seemed approaching ever nearer; a soulless, heartless, and unjoyous laugh, like that of the loon, solitary by the lakeside at midnight; a laugh which culminated in an unearthly shout close at hand, then died away by slow gradations, as if the accursed being that uttered it had withdrawn over the verge of the world whence it had come. But the man felt that this was not so—that it was nearby and had not moved.

A strange sensation began slowly to take possession of his body and his mind. He could not have said which, if any, of his senses were affected; he felt it rather as a consciousness—a mysterious mental assurance of some overpowering presence—some supernatural malevolence different in kind from the invisible existences that swarmed about him and superior to them in power. He knew that it had uttered that hideous laugh. And now it seemed to be approaching him; from what direction he did not know—dared not conjecture. All his former fears were forgotten or merged in the gigantic terror that now held him in thrall. Apart from that, he had but one thought: to complete his written appeal to the benign powers who, traversing the haunted wood, might some time rescue him if he should be denied the blessing of annihilation. He wrote with terrible rapidity, the twig in his fingers rilling blood without renewal; but in the middle of a sentence his hands denied their service to his will, his arms fell to his sides, the book to the earth; and powerless to move or cry out, he found himself staring into the sharply drawn face and blank, dead eyes of his own mother, standing white and silent in the garments of the grave.

II

In his youth Halpin Frayser had lived with his parents in Nashville, Tennessee. The Fraysers were well-to-do, having a good position in such society as had survived the wreck wrought by civil war. Their children had the social and educational opportunities of their time and place, and had responded to good associations and instruction with agreeable manners and cultivated minds. Halpin, being the youngest and not over-robust, was perhaps a trifle "spoiled." He had the double disadvantage of a mother's assiduity and a father's neglect.

Frayser *père* was what no Southern man of means is not—a politician. His country, or rather his section and state, made demands upon his time and attention so exacting that to those of his family he was compelled to turn an ear partly deafened by the thunder of the political captains and the shouting, his own included.

Young Halpin was of a dreamy, indolent and rather romantic turn, somewhat more addicted to literature than law, the profession to which he was bred. Among those of his relations who professed the modern faith of heredity it was well understood that in him the character of the late Myron Bayne, a maternal great-grandfather, had revisited the glimpses of the moon—by which orb Bayne had in his lifetime been sufficiently affected to be a poet of no small Colonial distinction. If not specially observed, it was observable that while a Frayser who was not the proud possessor of a sumptuous copy of the ancestral "poetical works" (printed at the family expense, and long ago withdrawn from an inhospitable market) was a rare Frayser indeed, there was an illogical indisposition to honor the great deceased in the person of his spiritual successor. Halpin was pretty generally deprecated as an intellectual black sheep who was likely at any moment to disgrace the flock by bleating in meter. The Tennessee Fraysers were a practical folk—not practical in the popular sense of devotion to sordid pursuits, but having a robust contempt for any qualities unfitting a man for the wholesome vocation of politics.

In justice to young Halpin it should be said that while in him were pretty faithfully reproduced most of the mental and moral characteristics ascribed by history and family tradition to the famous Colonial bard, his succession to the gift and faculty divine was purely inferential. Not only had he never been known to court the muse, but in truth he could not have written correctly a line of verse to save himself from the Killer of the Wise. Still, there was no knowing when the dormant faculty might wake and smite the lyre.

In the meantime the young man was rather a loose fish, anyhow. Between him and his mother was the most perfect sympathy, for secretly the lady was herself a devout disciple of the late and great Myron Bayne, though with the tact so generally and justly admired in her sex (despite the hardy calumniators who insist that it is essentially the same thing as cunning), she had always taken care to conceal her weakness from all eyes but those of him who shared it. Their common guilt in respect of that was an added tie between them. If in Halpin's youth his mother had "spoiled" him, he had assuredly done his part toward being spoiled. As he grew to such manhood as is attainable by a Southerner who does not care which way elections go, the attachment between him and his beautiful mother—whom from early childhood he had called Katy—became yearly stronger and more tender. In these two romantic natures was manifest in a signal way that neglected phenomenon, the dominance of the sexual element in all the relations of life, strengthening, softening, and beautifying even those of consanguinity. The two were nearly inseparable, and by strangers observing their manner were not infrequently mistaken for lovers.

Entering his mother's boudoir one day Halpin Frayser kissed her upon the forehead, toyed for a moment with a lock of her dark hair which had escaped from its confining pins, and said, with an obvious effort at calmness:

"Would you greatly mind, Katy, if I were called away to California for a few weeks?"

It was hardly needful for Katy to answer with her lips a question to which her telltale cheeks had made instant reply. Evidently she would greatly mind; and the tears, too, sprang into her large brown eyes as corroborative testimony.

"Ah, my son," she said, looking up into his face with infinite tenderness, "I should have known that this was coming. Did I not lie awake a half of the night weeping because, during the other half,

Grandfather Bayne had come to me in a dream, and standing by his portrait—young, too, and handsome as that—pointed to yours on the same wall? And when I looked it seemed that I could not see the features; you had been painted with a face cloth, such as we put upon the dead. Your father has laughed at me, but you and I, dear, know that such things are not for nothing. And I saw below the edge of the cloth the marks of hands on your throat—forgive me, but we have not been used to keep such things from each other. Perhaps you have another interpretation. Perhaps it does not mean that you will go to California. Or maybe you will take me with you?"

It must be confessed that this ingenious interpretation of the dream in the light of newly discovered evidence did not wholly commend itself to the son's more logical mind; he had, for the moment at least, a conviction that it foreshadowed a more simple and immediate, if less tragic, disaster than a visit to the Pacific Coast. It was Halpin Frayser's impression that he was to be garroted on his native heath.

"Are there not medicinal springs in California?" Mrs. Frayser resumed before he had time to give her the true reading of the dream. "Places where one recovers from rheumatism and neuralgia? Look— my fingers feel so stiff; and I am almost sure they have been giving me great pain while I slept."

She held out her hands for his inspection. What diagnosis of her case the young man may have thought it best to conceal with a smile the historian is unable to state, but for himself he feels bound to say that fingers looking less stiff, and showing fewer evidences of even insensible pain, have seldom been submitted for medical inspection by even the fairest patient desiring a prescription of unfamiliar scenes.

The outcome of it was that of these two odd persons, having equally odd notions of duty, the one went to California, as the interest of his client required, and the other remained at home in compliance with a wish that her husband was scarcely conscious of entertaining.

. While in San Francisco, Halpin Frayser was walking one dark night along the waterfront of the city, when, with a suddenness that surprised and disconcerted him, he became a sailor. He was in fact "shanghaied" aboard a gallant, gallant ship, and sailed for a far country. Nor did his misfortunes end with the voyage; for the ship was cast ashore on an island of the South Pacific, and it was six years afterward when the survivors were taken off by a venturesome trading schooner and brought back to San Francisco.

Though poor in purse, Frayser was no less proud in spirit than he had been in the years that seemed ages and ages ago. He would accept no assistance from strangers, and it was while living with a fellow survivor near the town of St. Helena, awaiting news and remittances from home, that he had gone gunning and dreaming.

III

The apparition confronting the dreamer in the haunted wood—the thing so like, yet so unlike his mother—was horrible! It stirred no love nor longing in his heart; it came unattended with pleasant memories of a golden past; inspired no sentiment of any kind; all the finer emotions were swallowed up in fear. He tried to turn and run from before it, but his legs were as lead; he was unable to lift his feet from the ground. His arms hung helpless at his sides; of his eyes only he retained control, and these he dared not remove from the lusterless orbs of the apparition, which he knew was not a soul without a body, but that most dreadful of all existences infesting that haunted wood—a body without a soul! In its blank stare was neither love, nor pity, nor intelligence—nothing to which to address an appeal for mercy. "An appeal will not lie," he thought, with an absurd reversion to professional slang, making the situation more horrible, as the fire of a cigar might light up a tomb.

For a time, which seemed so long that the world grew gray with age and sin, and the haunted forest, having fulfilled its purpose in this monstrous culmination of its terrors, vanished out of his consciousness with all its sights and sounds, the apparition stood within a pace, regarding him with the mindless malevolence of a wild brute; then thrust its hands forward and sprang upon him with appalling ferocity! The act released his physical energies without unfettering his will; his mind was still spellbound, but his powerful body and agile limbs, endowed with a blind, insensate life of their own, resisted stoutly and well. For an instant he seemed to see this unnatural contest between a dead intelligence and a breathing mechanism only as a spectator— such fancies are in dreams; then he regained his identity almost as if by a leap forward into his body, and the straining automaton had a directing will as alert and fierce as that of its hideous antagonist.

But what mortal can cope with a creature of his dream? The imagination creating the enemy is already vanquished; the combat's result is the combat's cause. Despite his struggles—despite his strength and activity, which seemed wasted in a void, he felt the cold fingers close upon his throat. Borne backward to the earth, he saw above him the dead and drawn face within a hand's breadth of his own, and then all was black. A sound as of the beating of distant drums—a murmur of swarming voices, a sharp, far cry signing all to silence, and Halpin Frayser dreamed that he was dead.

IV

A warm, clear night had been followed by a morning of drenching fog. At about the middle of the afternoon of the preceding day a little whiff of light vapor—a mere thickening of the atmosphere, the ghost of a cloud—had been observed clinging to the western side of Mount St. Helena, away up along the barren altitudes near the summit. It was so thin, so diaphanous, so like a fancy made visible, that one would have said: "Look quickly! In a moment it will be gone."

In a moment it was visibly larger and denser. While with one edge it clung to the mountain, with the other it reached farther and farther out into the air above the lower slopes. At the same time it extended itself to north and south, joining small patches of mist that appeared to come out of the mountainside on exactly the same level, with an intelligent design to be absorbed. And so it grew and grew until the summit was shut out of view from the valley, and over the valley itself was an ever-extending canopy, opaque and gray. At Calistoga, which lies near the head of the valley and the foot of the mountain, there was a starless night and a sunless morning. The fog, sinking into the valley, had reached southward, swallowing up ranch after ranch, until it had blotted out the town of St. Helena, nine miles away. The dust in the road was laid; trees were adrip with moisture; birds sat silent in their coverts; the morning light was wan and ghastly, with neither color nor fire.

Two men left the town of St. Helena at the first glimmer of dawn and walked along the road northward up the valley toward Calistoga. They carried guns on their shoulders, yet no one having knowledge of such matters could have mistaken them for hunters of bird or beast. They were a deputy sheriff from Napa and a detective from San Francisco—Holker and Jaralson, respectively. Their business was man-hunting.

"How far is it?" inquired Holker, as they strode along, their feet stirring white the dust beneath the damp surface of the road.

"The White Church? Only a half mile farther," the other answered. "By the way," he added, "it is neither white nor a church; it is an abandoned schoolhouse, gray with age and neglect. Religious services were once held in it when it was white, and there is a graveyard that would delight a poet. Can you guess why I sent for you, and told you to come heeled?"

"Oh! I never have bothered you about things of that kind. I've always found you communicative when the time came. But if I may hazard a guess, you want me to help you arrest one of the corpses in the graveyard."

"You remember Branscom?" said Jaralson, treating his companion's wit with the inattention that it deserved.

"The chap who cut his wife's throat? I ought; I wasted a week's work on him and had my expenses for my trouble. There is a reward of 500 dollars, but none of us ever got a sight of him. You don't mean to say—"

"Yes, I do. He has been under the noses of you fellows all the time. He comes by night to the old graveyard at the White Church."

"The devil! That's where they buried his wife."

"Well, you fellows might have had sense enough to suspect that he would return to her grave sometime."

"The very last place that anyone would have expected him to return to."

"But you had exhausted all the other places. Learning your failure at them, I 'laid for him' there."

"And you found him?"

"Damn it! he found me. The rascal got the drop on me—regularly held me up and made me travel. It's God's mercy that he didn't go through me. Oh, he's a good one, and I fancy the half of that reward is enough for me if you're needy."

Holker laughed good humoredly and explained that his creditors were never more importunate.

"I wanted merely to show you the ground and arrange a plan with you," the detective explained. "I thought it as well for us to be heeled, even in daylight."

"The man must be insane," said the deputy sheriff. "The reward is for his capture and conviction. If he's mad he won't be convicted."

Mr. Holker was so profoundly affected by that possible failure of justice that he involuntarily stopped in the middle of the road, then resumed his walk with abated zeal.

"Well, he looks it," assented Jaralson. "I'm bound to admit that a more unshaven, unshorn, unkempt, and uneverything wretch I never saw outside the ancient and honorable order of tramps. But I've gone in for him and can't make up my mind to let go. There's glory in it for us, anyhow. Not another soul knows that he is this side of the Mountains of the Moon."

"All right," Holker said, "we will go and view the ground," and he added, in the words of a once favorite inscription for tombstones: "'where you must shortly lie'—I mean, if old Branscom ever gets tired of you and your impertinent intrusion. By the way, I heard the other day that 'Branscom' was not his real name."

"What is?"

"I can't recall it. I had lost all interest in the wretch, and it did not fix itself in my memory—something like Pardee. The woman whose throat he had the bad taste to cut was a widow when he met her. She had come to California to look up some relatives—there are persons who will do that sometimes. But you know all that."

"Naturally."

"But not knowing the right name, by what happy inspiration did you find the right grave? The man who told me what the name was said it had been cut on the headboard."

"I don't know the right grave." Jaralson was apparently a trifle reluctant to admit his ignorance of so important a point of his plan. "I have been watching about the place generally. A part of our work this morning will be to identify that grave. Here is the White Church."

For a long distance the road had been bordered by fields on both sides, but now on the left there was a forest of oaks, madroños, and gigantic spruces whose lower parts only could be seen, dim and ghostly in the fog. The undergrowth was, in places, thick, but nowhere impenetrable. For some moments Holker saw nothing of the building, but as they turned into the woods, it revealed itself in faint gray outline through the fog, looking huge and far away. A few steps more, and it was within an arm's length, distinct, dark with moisture, and insignificant in size. It had the usual country-schoolhouse form—belonged to the packing-box order of architecture; had an underpinning of stones, a moss-grown roof, and blank window spaces, whence both glass and sash had long departed. It was ruined, but not a ruin—a typical Californian substitute for what are known to guide-bookers abroad as "monuments of the past." With scarcely a glance at this uninteresting structure Jaralson moved on into the dripping undergrowth beyond.

"I will show you where he held me up," he said. "This is the graveyard."

Here and there among the bushes were small enclosures containing graves, sometimes no more than one. They were recognized as graves by the discolored stones or rotting boards at head and foot, leaning at all angles, some prostrate; by the ruined picket fences surrounding them; or, infrequently, by the mound itself showing its gravel through the fallen leaves. In many instances nothing marked the spot where lay the vestiges of some poor mortal—who, leaving "a large circle of sorrowing friends," had been left by them in turn—except a depression in the earth, more lasting than that in the spirits of the mourners. The paths, if any paths had been, were long obliterated; trees of a considerable size had been permitted to grow up from the graves and thrust aside with root or branch the enclosing fences. Over all was that air of abandonment and decay which seems nowhere so fit and significant as in a village of the forgotten dead.

As the two men, Jaralson leading, pushed their way through the growth of young trees, that enterprising man suddenly stopped and brought up his shotgun to the height of his breast, uttered a low note of warning, and stood motionless, his eyes fixed upon something ahead. As well as he could, obstructed by brush, his companion, though seeing nothing, imitated the posture and so stood, prepared for what might ensue. A moment later Jaralson moved cautiously forward, the other following.

Under the branches of an enormous spruce lay the dead body of a man. Standing silent above it they noted such particulars as first strike the attention—the face, the attitude, the clothing; whatever most promptly and plainly answers the unspoken question of a sympathetic curiosity.

The body lay upon its back, the legs wide apart. One arm was thrust upward, the other outward; but the latter was bent acutely, and the hand was near the throat. Both hands were tightly clenched. The whole attitude was that of desperate but ineffectual resistance to—what?

Nearby lay a shotgun and a game bag through the meshes of which was seen the plumage of shot birds. All about were evidences of a furious struggle; small sprouts of poison-oak were bent and denuded of leaf and bark; dead and rotting leaves had been pushed into heaps and ridges on both sides of the legs by the action of other feet than theirs; alongside the hips were unmistakable impressions of human knees.

The nature of the struggle was made clear by a glance at the dead man's throat and face. While breast and hands were white, those were purple—almost black. The shoulders lay upon a low mound, and the head was turned back at an angle otherwise impossible, the expanded eyes staring blankly backward in a direction opposite to that of the feet. From the froth filling the open mouth the tongue protruded, black and swollen. The throat showed horrible contusions; not mere fingermarks, but bruises and lacerations wrought by two strong hands that must have buried themselves in the yielding flesh, maintaining their terrible grasp until long after death. Breast, throat, face were wet; the clothing was saturated; drops of water, condensed from the fog, studded the hair and mustache.

All this the two men observed without speaking—almost at a glance. Then Holker said:

"Poor devil! He had a tough deal."

Jaralson was making a vigilant circumspection of the forest, his shotgun held in both hands and at full cock, his finger upon the trigger.

"The work of a maniac," he said, without withdrawing his eyes from the enclosing wood. "It was done by Branscom—Pardee."

Something half-hidden by the disturbed leaves on the earth caught Holker's attention. It was a red-leather pocketbook. He picked it up and opened it. It contained leaves of white paper for memoranda, and upon the first leaf was the name "Halpin Frayser." Written in red on several succeeding leaves—scrawled as if in haste and barely legible were the following lines, which Holker read aloud, while his companion continued scanning the dim gray confines of their narrow world and hearing matter of apprehension in the drip of water from every burdened branch:

> "Enthralled by some mysterious spell, I stood
> In the lit gloom of an enchanted wood.
> The cypress there and myrtle twined their boughs,
> Significant, in baleful brotherhood.
>
> "The brooding willow whispered to the yew;
> Beneath, the deadly nightshade and the rue,
> With immortelles self-woven into strange
> Funereal shapes, and horrid nettles grew.
>
> "No song of bird nor any drone of bees,
> Nor light leaf lifted by the wholesome breeze:
> The air was stagnant all, and Silence was
> A living thing that breathed among the trees.
>
> "Conspiring spirits whispered in the gloom,
> Half-heard, the stilly secrets of the tomb.
> With blood the trees were all adrip; the leaves
> Shone in the witch-light with a ruddy bloom.

"I cried aloud!—the spell, unbroken still,
Rested upon my spirit and my will.
Unsouled, unhearted, hopeless and forlorn,
I strove with monstrous presages of ill!

"At last the viewless—"

Holker ceased reading; there was no more to read. The manuscript broke off in the middle of a line.

"That sounds like Bayne," said Jaralson, who was something of a scholar in his way. He had abated his vigilance and stood looking down at the body.

"Who's Bayne?" Holker asked rather incuriously.

"Myron Bayne, a chap who flourished in the early years of the nation—more than a century ago. Wrote mighty dismal stuff; I have his collected works. That poem is not among them, but it must have been omitted by mistake."

"It is cold," said Holker. "Let us leave here; we must have up the coroner from Napa."

Jaralson said nothing but made a movement in compliance. Passing the end of the slight elevation of earth upon which the dead man's head and shoulders lay, his foot struck some hard substance under the rotting forest leaves, and he took the trouble to kick it into view. It was a fallen headboard, and painted on it were the hardly decipherable words, "Catherine Larue."

"Larue, Larue!" exclaimed Holker, with sudden animation. "Why, that is the real name of Branscom—not Pardee. And—bless my soul! how it all comes to me—the murdered woman's name had been Frayser!"

"There is some rascally mystery here," said Detective Jaralson. "I hate anything of that kind."

There came to them from out of the fog—seemingly from a great distance—the sound of a laugh, a low, deliberate, soulless laugh, which had no more of joy than that of a hyena nightprowling in the desert; a laugh that rose by slow gradation, louder and louder, clearer, distinct and terrible, until it seemed more barely outside the narrow circle of their vision; a laugh so unnatural, so inhuman, so devilish, that it filled those hardy man-hunters with a sense of dread unspeakable! They did not move their weapons nor think of them; the menace of that horrible sound was not of the kind to be met with arms. As it had grown out of silence, so now it died away; from a culminating shout which had seemed almost in their ears, it drew itself away into the distance, until its failing notes, joyless and mechanical to the last, sank to silence at a measureless remove.

Navagating Four Horses
North of the Bay

Jack London

"Huh! Drive four horses! I wouldn't sit behind you—not for a thousand dollars—over them mountain roads."

So said Henry, and he ought to have known, for he drives four horses himself.

Said another Glen Ellen friend: "What? London? He drive four horses? Can't drive one!"

And the best of it is that he was right. Even after managing to get a few hundred miles with my four horses, I don't know how to drive one. Just the other day, swinging down a steep mountain road and rounding an abrupt turn, I came full tilt on a horse and buggy being driven by a woman up the hill. We could not pass on the narrow road, where was only a foot to spare, and my horses did not know how to

From Sunset Magazine, *no. 27, (Sept. 1911), p. 233–246.*

back, especially uphill. About 200 yards down the hill was a spot where we could pass. The driver of the buggy said she didn't dare back down because she was not sure of the brake. And as I didn't know how to tackle one horse, I didn't try it. So we unhitched her horse and backed down by hand. Which was very well, till it came to hitching the horse to the buggy again. She didn't know how. I didn't either, and I had depended on her knowledge. It took us about half an hour, with frequent debates and consultations, though it is an absolute certainty that never in its life was that horse hitched in that particular way.

No; I can't harness up one horse. But I can four, which compels me to back up again to get to my beginning. Having selected Sonoma Valley for our abiding place, Charmian and I decided it was about time we knew what we had in our own country and the neighboring ones. How to do it was the first question. Among our many weaknesses is the one of being old-fashioned. We don't mix with gasoline very well. And, as true sailors should, we naturally gravitate toward horses. Being one of those lucky individuals who carries his office under his hat, I should have to take a typewriter and a load of books along. This put saddle-horses out of the running. Charmian suggested driving a span. She had faith in me; besides, she could drive a span herself. But when I thought of the many mountains to cross and of crossing them for three months with a poor, tired span, I vetoed the proposition and said we'd have to come back to gasoline after all. This she vetoed just as emphatically, and a deadlock obtained until I received inspiration.

"Why not drive four horses?" I said.

"But you don't know how to drive four horses," was her objection.

I threw my chest out and my shoulders back. "What man has done, I can do," I proclaimed grandly. "And please don't forget that when we sailed on the *Snark* I knew nothing of navigation, and that I taught myself as I sailed."

"Very well," she said. (And there's faith for you!) "They shall be four saddle-horses, and we'll strap our saddles on behind the rig."

It was my turn to object. "Our saddle-horses are not broken to harness."

"Then break them."

And what I knew about horses, much less about breaking them, was just about as much as any sailor knows. Having been kicked, bucked off, fallen over backward upon, and thrown out and run over, on very numerous occasions, I had a mighty vigorous respect for horses; but a wife's faith must be lived up to, and I went at it.

King was a polo pony from St. Louis, and Prince a many-gaited love-horse from Pasadena. The hardest thing was to get them to dig in and pull. They frolicked along on the levels and galloped down the hills, but when they struck an up-grade and felt the weight of the breaking-cart, they stopped and turned around and looked at me. But I passed them, and my troubles began. Milda was fourteen years old, an unadulterated bronco, and in temperament was a combination of mule and jack-rabbit blended equally. If you pressed your hand on her flank and told her to get over, she lay down on you. If you got her by the head and told her to back, she walked forward over you. And if you got behind her and shoved and told her to "Giddap!" she sat down on you. Also, she wouldn't walk. For endless weary miles I strove with her, but never could I get her to walk a step. Finally, she was a manger-glutton. No matter how near or far from the stable, when six o'clock came around, she bolted for home and never missed the directest cross-road. Many times I rejected her.

The fourth and most rejected horse of all was the Outlaw. From the age of three to seven she had defied all horse-breakers and broken a number of them. Then a long, lanky cowboy, with a fifty-pound saddle and a Mexican bit, had got her proud goat. I was the next owner. She was my favorite riding-horse. Charmian said I'd have to put her in as a wheeler where I would have more control over her. Now Charmian had a favorite riding mare called Maid. I suggested

Maid as a substitute. Charmian pointed out that my mare was a branded range-horse, while hers was a thoroughbred, and that the legs of her mare would be ruined forever if she were driven for three months. I acknowledged her mare's thoroughbredness, and at the same time defied her to find any thoroughbred with as small and delicately-viciously pointed ears as my Outlaw. She indicated Maid's exquisitely thin shin bone. I measured the Outlaw's. It was equally thin, although, I insinuated, possibly more durable. This stabbed Charmian's pride. Of course her thoroughbred Maid, carrying the blood of "Old Lexington, Morella, and a streak of the super-enduring Morgan," could run, walk, and work my unregistered Outlaw into the ground; and that was the very precise reason why such a paragon of a saddle animal should not be degraded by harness.

So it was that Charmian remained obdurate, until, one day, I got her behind the Outlaw for a forty-mile drive. For every inch of those forty miles the Outlaw kicked and jumped, in between the kicks and jumps finding time and space in which to seize its teammate by the back of the neck and attempt to drag it to the ground. Another trick the Outlaw developed during that drive was suddenly to turn at right angles in the traces and endeavor to butt its teammate over the grade. Reluctantly and nobly did Charmian give in and consent to the use of Maid. The Outlaw's shoes were pulled off, and she was turned out on the range.

Finally, the four horses were hooked to the rig—a light Studebaker trap. With two hours and a half of practice, in which the excitement was not abated by several jack-poles and numerous kicking matches, I announced myself as ready for the start. Came the morning, and Prince, who was to have been a wheeler with Maid, showed up with a badly kicked shoulder. He did not exactly show up; we had to find him, for he was unable to walk. His leg swelled and continually swelled during the several days we waited for him. Remained only the Outlaw. In from pasture she came, shoes were nailed on, and she was harnessed into the wheel. Friends and relatives strove to press accident policies on me, but Charmian climbed up alongside, and Nakata got into the rear seat with the typewriter—Nakata, who sailed cabin-boy on the *Snark* for two years and who has shown himself afraid of nothing, not even of me and my amateur jamborees in experimenting with new modes of locomotion. And we did very nicely, thank you, especially after the first hour or so, during which time the Outlaw had kicked about fifty various times, chiefly to the damage of her own legs and the paintwork, and after she had bitten a couple of hundred times, to the damage of Maid's neck and Charmian's temper. It was hard enough to have her favorite mare in the harness without also enduring the spectacle of its being eaten alive.

Our leaders were joys. King being a polo pony and Milda a rabbit, they rounded curves beautifully and darted ahead like coyotes out of the way of the wheelers. Milda's besetting weakness was a frantic desire not to have the lead-bar strike her hocks. When this happened, one of three things occurred: either she sat down on the lead-bar, kicked it up in the air until she got her back under it, or exploded in a straight-ahead, harness-disrupting jump. Not until she carried the lead-bar clean away and danced a breakdown on it and the traces did she behave decently. Nakata and I made the repairs with good old-fashioned bale-rope, which is stronger than wrought iron any time, and we went on our way.

In the meantime I was learning—I shall not say to tool a four-in-hand—but just simply to drive four horses. Now it is all right enough to begin with four work-horses pulling a load of several tons. But to begin with four light horses, all running, and a light rig that seems to outrun them—well, when things happen they happen quickly. My weakness was total ignorance. In particular, my fingers lacked training, and I made the mistake of depending on my eyes to handle the reins. This brought me up against a disastrous optical illusion. The bight of the off lead-line, being longer and heavier than that of the off wheel-line, hung lower. In a moment requiring quick action, I invariably mistook the two lines. Pulling on what I thought was the wheel-line, in order to straighten the team, I would see the leaders swing abruptly around into a jack-pole. Now for sensations of sheer impotence, nothing can compare with a jack-pole, when the horrified driver beholds his leaders prancing gaily up the road and his wheelers jogging steadily down the road, all at the same time and all harnessed together and to the same rig.

I no longer jack-pole, and I don't mind admitting how I got out of the habit. It was my eyes that enslaved my fingers into ill practices. So I shut my eyes and let the fingers go it alone. Today my fingers are independent of my eyes and work automatically. I do not see what my fingers do. They just do it. All I see is the satisfactory result.

Still we managed to get over the ground that first day—down sunny Sonoma Valley to the old town to Sonoma, founded by General Vallejo as the remotest outpost on the northern frontier for the purpose of holding back the Gentiles, as the wild Indians of those days were called. Here history was made. Here the last Spanish mission was reared; here the Bear flag was raised; and here Kit Carson, and Fremont, and all our early adventurers, came and rested in the days before the days of gold.

We swung on over the low rolling hills, through miles of dairy farms and chicken ranches where every blessed hen is white, and down the slopes to Petaluma Valley. Here, in 1776, Captain Quiros came up Petaluma Creek from San Pablo Bay in quest of an outlet to Bodega Bay on the coast. And here, later, the Russians, with Alaskan hunters, carried skin boats across from Fort Ross to poach for sea otters on the Spanish preserve of San Francisco Bay. Here too, still later, General Vallejo built a fort, which still stands—one of the finest examples of Spanish adobe that remain to us. And here at the old fort, to bring the chronicle up to date, our horses proceeded to make peculiarly personal history with astonishing success and dispatch. King, our peerless polo-pony leader, went lame. So hopelessly lame did he go that no expert, then and afterward could determine whether the lameness was in his frogs, hoofs, legs shoulders, or head. Maid picked up a nail and began to limp. Milda, figuring the day already sufficiently spent and maniacal with manger gluttony, began to rabbit-jump. All that held her was the bale-rope. And the Outlaw, game to the last, exceeded all previous exhibitions of skin-removing, paint-marring, and horse-eating.

At Petaluma we rested over while King was returned to the ranch and Prince sent to us. Now Prince had proved himself an excellent wheeler, yet he had to go into the lead and let the Outlaw retain his old place. There is an axiom that a good wheeler is a poor leader. I object to the last adjective. A good wheeler makes an infinitely worse kind of a leader than that. I know...now. I ought to know. Since that day I have driven Prince a few hundred miles in the lead. He is neither any better nor any worse than the first mile he ran in the lead; and his worst is even extremely worse than what you are thinking. Not that he is vicious. He is merely a good-natured rogue who shakes hands for sugar, steps on your toes out of sheer excessive friendliness, and just goes on loving you in your harshest moments.

But he won't get out of the way. Also, whenever he is reproved for being in the wrong, he accuses Milda of it and bites the back of her neck. So bad has this become that whenever I yell "Prince!" in a loud voice, Milda immediately rabbit-jumps to the side, straight ahead, or sits down on the lead-bar. All of which is quite disconcerting. Picture it yourself. You are swinging a sharp, down-grade, mountain curve, at a fast trot. The rock wall is the outside of the curve. The inside of the curve is a precipice. The continuance of the curve is a narrow, unrailed bridge. You hit the curve, throwing the leaders in against the wall and making the pole-horse do the work. All is lovely. The leaders are hugging the wall like nestling doves. But the moment comes in the evolution when the leaders must shoot out ahead. They really must shoot, or else they'll hit the wall and miss the bridge. Also, behind them are the wheelers, and the rig, and you have just eased the brake in order to put sufficient snap into the maneuver. If ever teamwork is required, now is the time. Milda tries to shoot. She does her best, but

Prince, bubbling over with roguishness, lags behind. He knows the trick. Milda is half a length ahead of him. He times it to the fraction of a second. Maid, in the wheel, over-running him, naturally bites him. This disturbs the Outlaw, who has been behaving beautifully, and she immediately reaches across for Maid. Simultaneously, with a fine display of firm conviction that it's all Milda's fault, Prince sinks his teeth into the back of Milda's defenseless neck. The whole thing has occurred in less than a second. Under the surprise and pain of the bite, Milda either jumps ahead to the imminent peril of harness and lead-bar, or smashes into the wall, stops short with the lead-bar over her back, and emits a couple of hysterical kicks. The Outlaw in-variably selects this moment to remove paint. And after things are untangled and you have had time to appreciate the close shave, you go up to Prince and reprove him with your choicest vocabulary. And Prince, gazelle-eyed and tender, offers to shake hands with you for sugar. I leave it to any one: a boat would never act that way.

We have some history north of the bay. Nearly three centuries and a half ago, that doughty pirate and explorer, Sir Francis Drake, combing the Pacific for Spanish galleons, anchored in the bight formed by Point Reyes, on which today is one of the richest dairy regions in the world. Here, less than two decades after Drake, Sebastien Carmenon piled up on the rocks with a silkladen galleon from the Philippines. And in this same bay of Drake, long afterward, the Russian fur-poachers rendezvoused their *bidarkas* and stole in through the Golden Gate to the forbidden waters of San Francisco Bay.

Farther up the coast, in Sonoma County, we pilgrimaged to the sites of the Russian settlements. At Bodega Bay, south of what today is called Russian River, was their anchorage, while north of the river they built their fort. And much of Fort Ross still stands. Log bastions, church, and stables hold their own, and so well, with rusty hinges creaking, that we warmed ourselves at the hundred-years-old double fireplace and slept under the hand-hewn roof beams still held to-gether by spikes of hand-wrought iron.

We went to see where history had been made, and we saw scenery as well. One of our stretches in a day's drive was from beautiful Inverness on Tomales Bay, down the Olema Valley to Bolinas Bay, along the eastern shore of that body of water to Willow Camp, and up over the sea-bluffs, around the bastions of Tamalpais, and down to Sausalito. From the head of Bolinas Bay to Willow Camp the drive on the edge of the beach, and actually, for half-mile stretches, in the waters of the bay itself, was a delightful experience. The wonderful part was to come. Very few San Franciscans, much less Californians, know of that drive from Willow Camp, to the south and east along the poppy-blown cliffs, with the sea thundering in the sheer depths hundreds of feet below and the Golden Gate opening up ahead, disclosing smoky San Francisco on her many hills. Far off, blurred on the breast of the sea, can be seen the Farallones, which Sir Francis Drake passed on a southwest course in the thick of a fog that robbed him of the glory of discovering San Francisco Bay.

It was on this part of the drive that I decided at last I was learning real mountain-driving. To confess the truth, for delicious titillation of one's nerve, I have since driven over no mountain road that was worse, or better, rather, than that piece.

And then the contrast! From Sausalito, over excellent parklike boulevards, through the splendid redwoods and homes of Mill Valley, across the blossomed hills of Marin County, along the knoll-studded picturesque marshes, past San Rafael resting warmly among her hills, over the divide and up the Petaluma Valley, and on to the grassy feet of Sonoma Mountain and home. We covered fifty-five miles that day. Not so bad, eh, for Prince the rogue, the paint-removing Outlaw, the thin-shanked thoroughbred, and the rabbit-jumper? And they came in cool and dry, ready for their mangers and the straw.

Oh, we didn't stop. We considered we were just starting, and that was many weeks ago. We have kept on, going over six counties which are comfortably large, even for California, and we are still going. We have twisted and doubled, crisscrossed our tracks, made fascinating and lengthy dives into the interior valleys in the hearts of Napa and Lake counties, traveled the coast for hundreds of miles on end, and are now in Eureka, on Humboldt Bay, which was discovered by accident by the gold-seekers, who were trying to find their way to and from the Trinity diggings. Even here, the white man's history preceded them, for dim tradition says that the Russians once anchored here and hunted sea otter before the first Yankee trader rounded the Horn, or the first Rocky Mountain trapper thirsted across the "Great American Desert" and trickled down the snowy Sierra to the sun-kissed land. No; we are not resting our horses here on Humboldt Bay. We are writing this, gorging on abalones and mussels, digging clams, and catching record-breaking sea trout and rock cod in the intervals in which we are not sailing, motorboating, and swimming in the most temperately equable climate we have ever experienced.

These comfortably large counties! They are veritable empires. Take Humboldt, for instance. It is three times as large as Rhode Island, one and one-half times as large as Delaware, almost as large as Connecticut, and half as large as Massachusetts. The pioneer has done his work in this north-of-the-bay region, the foundations are laid, and all is ready for the inevitable inrush of population and adequate development of resources which so far have been no more than skimmed, and casually and carelessly skimmed at that. This region of the six counties alone will some day support a population of millions. In the meanwhile, O you homeseekers, you wealth-seekers, and, above all, you climate-seekers, now is the time to get in on the ground floor.

Robert Ingersoll once said that the genial climate of California would in a fairly brief time evolve a race resembling the Mexicans, and that in two or three generations the Californians would be seen of a Sunday morning on their way to a cockfight with a rooster under each arm. Never was made a rasher generalization, based on so absolute an ignorance of facts. It is to laugh. Here is a climate that breeds vigor, with just sufficient geniality to prevent the expenditure of most of that vigor in fighting the elements. Here is a climate where a man can work 365 days in the year without the slightest hint of enervation, and where for 365 nights he must perforce sleep under blankets. What more can one say? I consider myself somewhat of a climate expert, having adventured among most of the climates of five out of the six zones. I have not yet been in the Antarctic, but whatever climate obtains there will not deter me from drawing the conclusion that nowhere is there a climate to compare with that of this region. Maybe I am as wrong as Ingersoll was. Nevertheless I take my medicine by continuing to live in this climate. Also, it is the only medicine I ever take.

But to return to the horses. There is some improvement. Milda has actually learned to walk. Maid has proved her thoroughbredness by never tiring on the longest days, and, while being the strongest and highest spirited of all, by never causing any trouble save for an occasional kick at the Outlaw. And the Outlaw rarely gallops, no longer butts, only periodically kicks, comes in to the pole and does her work without attempting to vivisect Maid's medulla oblongata, and—marvel of marvels—is really and truly getting lazy. But Prince remains the same incorrigible, loving, and lovable rogue as always.

And the country we've been over! The drives through Napa and Lake counties! One, from Sonoma Valley, via Santa Rosa, we could not refrain from taking several ways, and on all the ways we found the roads excellent for machines as well as horses. One route, and a more delightful one for an automobile cannot be found, is out from Santa Rosa, past old Altruria and Mark West Springs, then to the right and across to Calistoga in Napa Valley. By keeping to the left, the drive holds on up the Russian River Valley, through the miles of the noted Asti vineyards to Cloverdale, and then by way of Pieta, Witter, and Highland Springs to Lakeport. Still another way we took was down Sonoma Valley, skirting San Pablo Bay, and up the lovely Napa Valley. From Napa were side excursions through Pope and Berryessa valleys, on to Aetna Springs, and into Lake County, crossing the famous Langtry Ranch.

More valley from Ukiah to Willits, and then we turned westward through the virgin Sherwood forest of magnificent redwood, stopping at Alpine for the night and continuing on through Mendocino County to Fort Bragg and "salt water." We also came to Fort Bragg up the coast from Fort Ross, keeping our coast journey intact from the Golden Gate. The coast weather was cool and delightful, the coast driving superb. Especially in the Fort Ross section did we find the roads thrilling, while all the way along we followed the sea. At every stream the road skirted dizzy cliff edges, dived down into lush growths of forest and ferns, and climbed out along the cliff edges again. The way was lined with flowers—wild lilac, wild roses, poppies, and lupins. Such lupins!—giant clumps of them of every lupin shade and color. And it was along the Mendocino roads that Charmian caused many delays by insisting on getting out to pick the wild blackberries, strawberries, and thimbleberries which grew so profusely. And ever we caught peeps, far down, of steam schooners loading lumber in the rocky coves; ever we skirted the cliffs, day after day, crossing stretches of rolling farm lands and passing through thriving villages and saw-mill towns. Memorable was our launch-trip from Mendocino City up Big River, where the steering gears of the launches work the reverse of anywhere else in the world; where we saw a stream of logs, of six to twelve and fifteen feet in diameter, which filled the riverbed for miles to the obliteration of any sign of water; and where we were told of a white or albino redwood tree. We did not see this last, so cannot vouch for it.

All the streams were filled with trout, and more than once we saw side-hill salmon on the slopes. No, side-hill salmon is not a peripatetic fish; it is a deer out of season. But the trout! At Gualala Charmian caught her first one. Once before in my life I had caught two...on angleworms. On occasion I had tried fly and spinner and never got a strike, and I had come to believe that all this talk of fly-fishing was just so much nature-faking. But on the Gualala River I caught trout—a lot of them—on fly and spinner; and I was beginning to feel quite an expert, until Nakata, fishing on bottom with a pellet of bread for bait, caught the biggest trout of all. I now affirm there is nothing in science nor in art. Nevertheless, since that day poles and baskets have been added to our baggage, we tackle every stream we come to, and we no longer are able to remember the grand total of our catch.

At Usal, many hilly and picturesque miles north of Fort Bragg, we turned again into the interior of Mendocino, crossing the ranges and coming out in Humboldt County on the south fork of Eel River at Garberville. Throughout the trip, from Marin County north, we had been warned of "bad roads ahead." Yet we never found those bad roads. We seemed always to be just ahead of them or behind them. The farther we came the better the roads seemed, though this was probably due to the fact that we were learning more and more what four horses and a light rig could do on a road. And thus do I save my face with all the counties. I refuse to make invidious road comparisons. I can add that while, save in rare instances on steep pitches, I have trotted my horses down all the grades, I have never had one horse fall down nor have I had to send the rig to a blacksmith shop for repairs.

Also, I am learning to throw leather. If any tyro thinks it is easy to take a short-handled, long-lashed whip, and throw the end of that lash just where he wants it, let him put on automobile goggles and try it. On reconsideration, I would suggest the substitution of a wire fencing-mask for the goggles. For days I looked at that whip. It fascinated me, and the fascination was composed mostly of fear. At my first attempt, Charmian and Nakata became afflicted with the same fascination, and for a long time afterward, whenever they saw me reach for the whip, they closed their eyes and shielded their heads with their arms.

Here's the problem. Instead of pulling honestly, Prince is lagging back and maneuvering for a bite at Milda's neck. I have four reins in my hands. I must put these four reins into my left hand, properly gather the whip handle and the bight of the lash in my right hand, and throw that lash past Maid without striking her and into Prince. If the lash strikes Maid, her thoroughbredness will go up in the air, and I'll have a case of horse hysteria on my hands for the next half hour. But follow. The whole problem is not yet stated. Suppose that I miss Maid and reach the intended target. The instant the lash cracks, the four horses jump, Prince most of all, and his jump, with spread wicked teeth, is for the back of Milda's neck. She jumps to escape— which is her second jump, for the first one came when the lash exploded. The Outlaw reaches for Maid's neck, and Maid, who has already jumped and tried to bolt, tries to bolt harder. And all this infinitesimal fraction of time I am trying to hold the four animals with my left hand, while my whip-lash, writhing through the air, is coming back to me. Three simultaneous things I must do: keep hold of the four lines with my left hand; slam on the brake with my foot; and on the rebound catch that flying lash in the hollow of my right arm and get the bight of it safely into my right hand. Then I must get two of the four lines back into my right hand and keep the horses from running away or going over the grade. Try it some time. You will find life anything but wearisome. Why, the first time I hit the mark and made the lash go off like a revolver shot, I was so astounded and delighted that I was paralyzed. I forgot to do any of the multitudinous other things, tangled the whip-lash in Maid's harness, and was forced to call upon Charmian for assistance. And now, confession. I carry a few pebbles handy. They're great for reaching Prince in a tight place. But just the same I'm learning that whip every day, and before I get home I hope to discard the pebbles. And as long as I rely on pebbles, I cannot truthfully speak of myself as "tooling a four-in-hand."

From Garberville, where we ate eel to repletion and got acquainted with the aborigines, we drove down the Eel River Valley for two days through the most unthinkably glorious body of redwood timber to be seen anywhere in California. From Dyerville on to Eureka we caught glimpses of railroad construction and of great concrete bridges in the course of building, which advertised that at last Humboldt County is to be linked to the rest of the world.

We still consider our trip is just begun. As soon as this is mailed from Eureka, it's "heigh-ho!" for the horses and pull on. We shall continue up the coast, turn in for the Hoopa Reservation and the gold mines, and shoot down the Trinity and Klamath rivers in Indian canoes to Requa. After that, we shall go on through Del Norte County and into Oregon. The trip so far has justified us in taking the attitude that we won't go home until the winter rains drive us in. And, finally, I am going to try the experiment of putting the Outlaw in the lead and relegating Prince to his old position in the near wheel. I won't need any pebbles then.

from They Knew What They Wanted

Sidney Howard

Act One

*T*he red, white, and green of Italy combine with the red, white, and blue of these United States in bunting, garlands of fluted paper, pompons, and plumes of shredded tissue, to make up a scheme of decoration which is, to say the least, violent. The picture of Garibaldi is draped with an American flag. The picture of Washington with an Italian flag. The full glare of the early morning sun streams in through door and windows.

The room is fairly littered with boxes. Atop one of these, from which it has just been extracted, stands a handsome wedding cake, surmounted by statuary representing the ideal bride and groom in full regalia under a bell. The boxes are all addressed to Tony Patucci, R.F.D., Napa, Calif.

AH GEE *stands on a ladder on the porch outside the open entrance door, hanging Chinese lanterns. He is a silent, spare Chinaman, of age maturely indeterminate. He wears blue overalls and a black chambray shirt.*

JOE—*dark, sloppy, beautiful, and young—is busy opening a packing case in the center of the stage. His back is turned upon the door.*

JOE *(As he works, he half sings, half mutters to himself the words of "Remember,"an I.W.W. song, to the tune of "Hold the Fort.")*

"We speak to you from jail today,
Two hundred union men,
We're here because the bosses' laws
Bring slavery again."

(Through this the curtain rises and FATHER MCKEE *is seen climbing the porch steps. He wears the sober garb of a Catholic priest, not over clean, what with dust, spots, and all. He nods to* AH GEE *and comes into the doorway. He stands a moment to mop his large, pale face with a red bandana. Then he lowers his lugubrious disapproval upon everything in sight. Then he yawns.*

He is one of those clerics who can never mention anything except to denounce it. And his technique of denunciation is quite special to himself. It consists of a long, throaty abstention from inflexion of any kind which culminates in a vocal explosion when he reaches the accented syllable of the word upon which his emphasis depends. This word always seems to wake him up for an instant. Once it is spoken, however, he relapses into semi-somnolence for the remainder of his remarks. At heart, he is genial and kindly enough, quite the American counterpart of the French village curé.*)*

FATHER MCKEE: Hello, Joe.

JOE: Hello there, Padre. What do you think?

FATHER MCKEE: Looks to me like a bawdy house.

JOE: It's goin' to be *some* festa....Lily Cups! What do you know about
    that for style?

FATHER MCKEE: Where's Tony?

JOE (*Nods toward the door of the bedroom*): In there gettin' dolled up
    ....Hey, there, bridegroom! The Padre's out here.

FATHER MCKEE: I come up to have a serious talk with Tony.

JOE: Well, for God's sake, don't get him upset no more'n what he is
    already. He's been stallin' around all mornin', afraid to go down
    and meet the bride. You better leave him alone.

FATHER MCKEE: I'm always glad to have your advice, Joe. I didn't
    look to find you still hangin' 'round.

JOE: Oh, didn't you, Padre?

FATHER MCKEE: Tony told me you'd decided to go away.

JOE: Well, Padre, I'll tell you how it is. (*He grins imprudently.*) I don't
    believe in stayin' any one place too long. 'T'ain't fair for me not
    to give the rest of California a chance at my society. But I ain't
    goin' before I seen all the fun, got Tony safely married, an' kissed
    the bride. (*He turns to the door and AH GEE.*) That's fine, Ah Gee.
    Better take these here Lily Cups in the kitchen when you get
    through.

    (*Magnificently TONY enters from the bedroom. He is stout, floridly
bronzed, sixty years old, vigorous, jovial, simple, and excitable. His great gift is for
gesture. Today we meet him in his Sunday best, a very brilliant purple suit with a
more than oriental waistcoat which serves to display a stupendous gold watch chain.
He wears a boiled shirt, an emerald green tie, and a derby hat. He carries his new
patent-leather shoes in his hand. He seems to be perspiring rather freely.*)

TONY: Looka me! I'm da most stylish fella in da world.

FATHER McKEE: I come up to talk to you, Tony.

TONY: I'm glad you come, Padre. How you like my clothes, eh? Costa playnta good money! (*Attention is called to the shoes.*) For da feet....

JOE (*A motion to the wedding cake*): How's it strike you, Tony?

TONY: Madonna! (*He throws his shoes into the morris chair. His hat assumes a terrific angle. He cannot keep his hands off that cake.*) Look, Padre! From Frisco! Special! Twelve dollar' an' two bits! Look! (*The miniature bride and groom particularly please him.*) Ees Tony an' his Amy!

JOE: Them lanterns is Ah Gee's personal donation.

TONY: Thank you, Ah Gee! Ees verra fine. Ah Gee, you go an' bring vino, now, for Padre, eh? (AH GEE *obeys the order, taking the Lily Cups with him into his kitchen.*)

JOE: Show some speed now, Tony. It's past nine. 'T'ain't hardly pretty to keep the bride waitin'.

TONY (*As he sits down to struggle with his shoes*): I'm goin' verra quick.

FATHER McKEE: I got to have a word with you, Tony, before you go to the station.

JOE: The Padre's been tryin' to tell me you're scared to have me around where I can kiss the bride. (*He picks up a couple of flags and goes outside.*)

TONY (*In undisguised terror*): You ain' goin' be kissin' no bride, Joe. You hear dat?

JOE (*Off stage he is heard singing*):

"We laugh and sing, we have no fear
Our hearts are always light,
We know that every Wobbly true
Will carry on the fight."

TONY: He's too goddam fresh, dat fella, with kissin' my Amy an' all dose goddam Wobbly songs. Don' you think so, Padre?

FATHER MCKEE: I didn't come up here to talk about Joe, Tony. I come up to talk about this here weddin'.

TONY: I'm glad you come, Padre. I'm verra bad scare'.

FATHER MCKEE: You got good reason for bein' scared, if you want to know what *I* think.

TONY: I got verra special reason.

FATHER MCKEE: What reason?

TONY: Don' you never mind! Da's my secret dat I don' tell nobody. You tell Joe he go away quick, Padre. Den, maybe, ees all right.

FATHER MCKEE: So that's it! Well, I don't blame you for that.

TONY (*Deeply indignant at the implication*): Oh!...No, by God! You don' ondrastan', Padre. Joe is like my own son to me! Ees som'thing verra different. Madonna mia! Ees som'thing I been doin' myself! Ees som'thing Tony's been doin' w'at's goin' mak' verra bad trouble for Tony.

FATHER MCKEE: I'll tell Joe nothin'. You've made your own bed and if you won't get off it while there's time, you got to lie on it. But I want you to understand that I don't like nothin' 'bout this here weddin'. It ain't got my approval.

TONY (*The first shoe slips on, and he sits up in amazement*): You don' like weddin', Padre?

FATHER MCKEE: No, I don't. An' that's just what I come up here to tell you. I don't like nothin' about it, an' if you persist in goin' ahead in spite of my advice, I don't want you sayin' afterwards that you wasn't warned.

TONY: Dio mio! (*He amplifies this with the sign of the cross. Then his confidence rather returns to him.*) Aw...tak' a pinch-a snuff! You mak' me tire', Padre! You think festa is no good for people. You padre fellas don' know nothing. Work! Work! Work evra day! Den, by-an'-by, is comin' festa. After festa workin' is more easy. (*He resumes the shoe problem.*)

FATHER MCKEE: Tony, you know perfectly well that I ain't got no more objection to no festa than I have to any other pomp of the flesh. But I'm your spirichool advisor an' I been mullin' this weddin' over in my mind an' I come to the conclusion that I'm agin it. I don't like it at all. I got my reasons for what I say.

TONY (*Does the Padre guess his secret?*): W'at reason you got?

FATHER MCKEE: In the first place, you ain't got no business marryin' no woman who ain't a good Cath'lic.

TONY (*Immeasurable relief*): Ees no matter.

FATHER MCKEE: A mixed marriage ain't no better'n plain livin' in sin.

TONY: Ain' we got you for keep sin away, Padre?

FATHER McKEE: Why ain't you marryin' a woman out of your own parish instead of trapesin' all the way to Frisco to pick out a heretic?

TONY: Is no good womans in dees parish.

FATHER McKEE: What's wrong with 'em?

TONY: Joe is sleepin' with evra one.

FATHER McKEE: That ain't the point.

TONY (*Enlisting the shoe to help his gesticulation*): Oh, ees point all right, Padre. Joe is told me 'bout evrathing. I been lookin' all 'round here at all da womans in dees parish. I been lookin' evra place for twent' mile. Ees no good womans for wife here. Joe is told me 'bout evra one. Den I'm gone to Napa for look all 'round dere, an' in Napa ees no better...ees just da same like here. So den I go down all da way to Frisco for look after wife an' I find my Amy. She is like a rose, all wilt'. You puttin' water on her an' she come out most beautiful. I'm goin' marry with my Amy, Padre, an' I don' marry with nobody else. She's been tellin' me she is no Cath'lic. I say, w'at I care? By-an'-by, maybe, if we bein' patient, we bringin' her in da church, an' showin' her da candles and da Madonna, all fix up good with flowers and da big tin heart, an' evrathing smellin' so prett' an' you preachin' verra loud an' da music an' evrathing, maybe....by-an'-by....(*He turns again to his shoe.*) But now ees no matter. W'at I care?

FATHER McKEE: It don't look good to me.

TONY: Ees, all right....If you don' want my Amy an' me gettin' married with good Cath'lic priest like you, den, by God—

FATHER McKEE: I ain't said I wouldn't marry you.

TONY: Eh bene!

FATHER McKEE: I'm only tryin' to tell you...

TONY: Ahi! Dio mio....(*The shoe goes on, producing intense pain.*) He look much better as he feel!

FATHER McKEE: There ain't no good in no old man marryin' with no young woman.

TONY: You think anybody marry with old woman? Tak' a pinch-a snuff!

FATHER McKEE: I know one old man who married a young woman an' she carried on with a stage driver!

TONY: Dio mio!

FATHER McKEE: He had knowed her all her life, too, an' you ain't knowed your Amy more'n 'bout five minutes.

TONY: Ees no matter.

FATHER McKEE: An' I know another fellow who married one of them city girls like your Amy without bein' properly acquainted, an' she turned out to be a scarlet woman.

TONY: My Amy don' do dat. (AH GEE *enters from kitchen with two glasses and a bottle of wine.*)

FATHER McKEE: Ain't you just now been tellin' me you're scared of her seein' Joe?

TONY: No, by God!

FATHER McKEE: Joe ain't the only young fellow around, either!

TONY: Young fellas is no matter. Only Joe. An' I ain' scare' over Joe excep' for special reason. You tell Joe, Padre...(*He is returning to his old subject, but the wine distracts him.*) Ah-h-h!

FATHER McKEE: Why didn't you get married forty years ago?

TONY: I think you know verra good w'y. Ees because I'm no dam' fool....W'en I'm young, I got nothing. I'm broke all da time, you remember? I got no money for havin' wife. I don' want no wife for mak' her work all da time. Da's no good, dat. Da's mak' her no more young, no more prett'. Evrabody say Tony is crazy for no' havin' wife. I say Tony is no dam' fool. W'at is happen? Pro'ibish' is com'. Salute! (*A glass of wine.* AH GEE *has returned to his kitchen.*) An w'at I say? I say, "Ees dam' fool law. Ees dam' fool fellas for bein' scare' an' pullin' up da grape' for tryin' growin' som'thing different." W'at I'm doin'? I'm keep the grape, eh? I say, "I come in dees country for growin' da grape! God mak' dees country for growin' da grape! Ees not for pro'ibish' God mak' dees country. Ees for growin' da grape!" Ees true? Sure ees true! (*Another glass of wine.*) An' w'at happen? Before pro'ibish' I sell my grape' for ten, maybe twelve dollar' da ton. Now I sell my grape' some'time one hundra dollar' da ton. Pro'ibish' is mak' me verra rich. (*Another glass of wine.*) I got my fine house. I got Joe for bein' foreman. I got two men for helpin' Joe. I got one Chink for cook. I got one Ford car. I got all I want, evrathing, excep' only wife. Now I'm goin' have wife. Verra nice an' young an' fat. Not for work. No! For sit an' holdin' da hands and havin' kids. Three kids. (*He demonstrates the altitude of each.*) Antonio...Giuseppe...Anna...Da's like trees an' cows an' all good peoples. Da's fine for God an' evrabody! I tell you, Padre, Tony know w'at he want!

FATHER MCKEE: Whatever made you think a man of your age could have children? (*This staggers* TONY.) I tell you, Tony, it ain't possible.

TONY: Eh? Tony is too old for havin' kids? I tell you, Tony can have twent' kids if he want! I tell you, Tony can have kids w'en he is one hundra year' old. Dio mio! From da sole of his feet to da top of his hat, Tony is big, strong man! I think I ondrastan' you verra good, Padre. Tony is not too old for havin' kids. He's too rich, eh? (*This rather strikes home.*) Yah! Tony is rich an' if he don' have no kids, den da church is gettin' all Tony's money an da Padre is gettin' Tony's fine house all fix' up good for livin' in, eh?

FATHER MCKEE (*A very severe shepherd*): Tony!

TONY (*The horns of the devil with his fingers*): Don' you go puttin' no evil eye on Tony an' his Amy!

FATHER MCKEE: You're givin' way to ignorant superstition, which ain't right in no good Cath'lic.

TONY (*On his feet in a panic*): Dio mio! My Amy is comin' on dat train an' here you keep me, sittin', talking...

FATHER MCKEE: You irreverent, old lunatic, you, if you're bent on marrin', I'll marry you. (JOE *reappears in the doorway.*) But I don't want you comin' around afterwards sqawkin' about it.

TONY: Eh, Joe! Da Padre don' want me gettin' marry with my Amy because he's scare' da church don' never get my money!

JOE: For cripe's sake, Tony, ain't you heard that whistle?

TONY: I go! I go!

JOE: Train's in now.

TONY: Porco Dio! Ah Gee!

JOE: fix your tie.

TONY: I fix....(AH GEE *comes from the kitchen for his master's order.*) Un altro fiasco. (AH GEE *returns to the kitchen.*)

JOE: You won't make no hit if you're drunk, Tony.

TONY: Not drunk, Joe. Only scare'. Verra bad scare'.

JOE: Bridegrooms is always scared.

TONY: Jes' Chris', maybe I'm sick!

JOE: No!

TONY: Santa Maria! I *am* sick!

JOE: What's wrong with you?

TONY: I don' know! I'm sick! I'm sick! I'm sick! (AH GEE *returns with the wine bottle refilled* TONY *seeks prompt solace.* AH GEE *goes back to his kitchen.*)

JOE: You'll be a helluva sight sicker if you don't lay off that stuff.

TONY: I canno' go for get my Amy, Joe. I canno' go....

JOE: All right I'll go....

TONY: Oh, by God! No! NO!

JOE: Tony, if you drive the Ford down the hill in this state of mind, you'll break your dam' neck.

TONY (*More solace*): I feel good now. I drive fine. I don' want nobody for go for my Amy but only me....(*Then he weakens again.*) Joe, I'm scare', I'm scare', I'm scare'!

JOE: What you scared of, Tony?

TONY: Maybe my Amy....

JOE: Come on, beat it!

TONY: I feel good now an' I don' want nobody for go for my Amy but only me. You bet! (*He starts.*)

Miss Peake

Frances Marion

Today the spirit of Miss Peake is in my garden hovering gently over Sam Tuttle and me as we sit under the silver aspen, reviving old memories and long forgotten dreams. He knew Miss Peake, and he visions her sweetly, delicately, and with infinite tenderness.

One would not associate Mr. Sam Tuttle, the county schoolhouse painter, with romance. He is a drab little soul, gray as a mouse. Thin spears of hair rise sparsely from his gleaming dome of a head. His eyes are dewy with age and loneliness.

His voice cracks and quivers at times as he tells me of Miss Peake.

From Valley People. *Copyright © 1935 by Frances Marion. Published by Reynal & Hitchcock, New York.*

There was something about Miss Peake that made me like her the first time I went to work painting the old schoolhouse. Not many teachers would have had time to say more than "Good morning!" to a school painter, but Miss Peake did. We became very good friends after that week she was away sick and came back to find that I'd watered the plant on the windowsill in back of her desk. Elmira Fink, the monitor, promised to water it, but I guess she forgot. Miss Peake thought a great deal of that little plant.

"It's not an ordinary nasturtium, Mr. Tuttle," she said. "You'll see that when it blooms. It's a double one and quite rare."

"Is that so, Miss Peake? Well, well, well, I don't think I've ever seen a double nasturtium."

Miss Peake's mouth always puckered a little. Perhaps she held her upper lip so tight over her front teeth that it had set that way. There were funny little grooves running to her mouth, which seemed tucked in a little. But I liked her mouth, which wasn't like some of the young Valley girls', all smeared with scarlet paint.

I'm a man who could never bear to see one of God's children paint her face like a Jezebel. I told Miss Peake so, when we became a little more friendly. And she was pleased, too. "You're right, Mr. Tuttle," she said to me, pushing a lock of her thin straight hair off her forehead. "I guess I'm what you might call old-fashioned."

"You are, Miss Peake, and bless you for it," I said. "It fits into a noble educational environment like this, where a woman should have dignity. I can never bear to look at a teacher sitting with a painted face and her hair flying in all directions on her head, right in front of young children. It mortifies me to see shiny fingernails snatching at the Bible when they open school, mornings. Some teachers have no respect for the sacred volume, either. Why, do you know, in the Calistoga school, I saw a piece of gum sticking to a corner of the King James Version and, sure enough, there in the basket under that teacher's desk were the wrappers of it!"

"Oh, surely, Mr. Tuttle, not gum!"

"But that isn't all, Miss Peake. Every night there was face powder spilled all over her desk, and once I caught her looking, without shame, at the naked picture of a prize fighter. 'There's a man for you, Tuttle,' she said, and she smacked her lips so loud I was afraid the children would hear it."

Miss Peake always blushed in little red spots all over her neck, and I knew I'd been too indelicate. "Not entirely naked," I hastened to explain, "but there was such a small part of him covered that no respectable lady should have looked at a picture like that in public."

I didn't dream at that time that Elmira Fink, the oldest girl in the school, had put a photograph of a man, most as bad as that, on Miss Peake's desk between the covers of her geography.

The story of what Elmira Fink had done spread through the Valley, and her ma gave her the devil. With my own ears, I heard Elmer Larson laugh about it.

"Don't laugh at Miss Peake, Elmer, the poor thing never had a chance in life," said Doctor Griswold, and it burned me up to hear him speak that way about Miss Peake, just because she didn't wear dresses that showed what the Lord intended only for the eyes of a husband.

"What she needs is a man!" Elmer Larson said right out.

"Poor old maid!" said Doctor Griswold.

I coughed to let them know I overheard them. I didn't care a whit if Doctor Griswold didn't like it, I wasn't going to be a party to such loose talk, and I was tempted for a moment to say something, but a man in Doctor Griswold's position, head of the School Board, too, isn't one to take any reproval from a school painter, and after all, these were very hard times, and I had been out of work the best part of two years.

When the double nasturtium bloomed, Miss Peake called me in to look at it. She clasped her thin hands, and her face seemed to shine as if a light had been turned on inside her.

"Oh, Mr. Tuttle, I was so afraid they wouldn't mature," she said, as if she were speaking of children. *Her* children, I thought to

myself, and I was ashamed of my familiarity. "Aren't they beautiful?"
she said, and she leaned over to look more closely at them, for she had
left her thick glasses on the desk. "Do you know what they remind
me of?"

"Nothing but flowers," I said.

"They're like a party dress!" she cried, with a queer kind of
excitement. "A gold party dress, all flaring ruffles at the bottom and
showing little green slippers and green silk...."

But she stopped right there, and I noticed those red spots came
out on her neck again. Miss Peake wasn't like some of the Valley girls;
she couldn't bring herself to speak about stockings to a gentlemen,
when stockings suggested nothing else but a woman's legs. Our hands
touched as we stood there and looked at the nasturtiums. Not boldly.
I don't want you to misunderstand my feelings for Miss Peake, but
just lightly, as hands meet hands when you dream. But when I looked
at her, I must say that I found her very pleasing, and after knowing her
that close, I couldn't bear to have Miss Peake think of me only as a
school painter.

"I am a musician," I said to her one day after school.

"Really! A pianist?"

"No. But I play the oboe fairly well," I answered, trying not to
appear vain. "I played it fourteen years in an orchestra at the old Tivoli
Opera House in San Francisco."

"Why, Mr. Tuttle, how exciting! You must have seen quite a bit
of life then."

"Indeed I did, Miss Peake." But I was glad that she couldn't read
my mind, for it had become alive with memories that were not
entirely delicate.

"Why, I didn't dream you'd had such a past!"

"I suppose it could be called a past," and I hastened to assure her
that when they brought their vulgar Gilbert and Sullivan comedies to
take the place of the delightful old operas, I was forced to resign.
Shortly after, I became an Evangelist, and once I was arrested for

venturing into the Barbary Coast to plead with the fallen men and women to pray because the world was coming to an end.

"I have never heard an oboe," said Miss Peake. "I mean, apart from an orchestra. What a pleasant experience you must have had sitting there night after night looking up at a beautiful stage, with all its gay people and bright colors. I'm sure I would have enjoyed it too much ever to have left it."

"Yes, you would, Miss Peake, you would!" I lowered my voice when I heard the squeak of Doctor Griswold's new boots coming up the steps. "Some of the chorus ladies had no morals. They smoked and drank and even painted their faces."

"But they were actresses, Mr. Tuttle."

"I mean, *off* the stage! And they went out with men they had no intention of marrying. Sometimes their actions were reprehensible. Even toward *me*, who had studied for the ministry before I took up my career with the oboe."

"Not with *you*, Mr. Tuttle!" I wasn't sure that she meant that for a compliment. It made me kind of wish that she had seen me before I lost most of my hair, but, of course, a man in his fifties can't expect to look as well as he did when he was only forty.

"I'd like to hear you play the oboe," she said politely, but I shook my head.

"I'm afraid I'm out of practice, Miss Peake. You see, it's been over twelve years since I've had my hands on one."

The next season, I suggested she get petunias instead of double nasturtiums, and I must admit I felt a little bit hurt when she thanked me for the petunia seeds and said she'd take them home with her.

"It's this way, Mr. Tuttle," as she explained it. "I can't get away from their gold party gowns. Sometimes, when there's a lull in my class, I like to imagine what fun it would be to have a gown, all flaring, with ruffles like the petals, with green slippers and lovely green stockings to match them."

You can see how our friendship was growing, for now Miss Peake could talk quite freely about stockings. But I began to worry for fear she was losing her memory a little, she told me so often her idea about the gold party dress. It did seem unreasonable that she couldn't remember she had told me that so many times.

Then one day, I'll never forget it! Miss Peake didn't stay an hour after school closed as she had done every day for years and years, but she rushed right through her reports, leaving papers every which way on her desk. She flew out of there without even stopping to say good-night to me!

I asked Elmira Fink, though I didn't like talking to her, if there had been a death in Miss Peake's family.

"Death, your grandmother!" she replied in her usual bold way. "Old Peake's come to life, that's all. She's gone clear to Napa to buy herself a party dress. Now have a laugh at *that!*"

A party dress! Well, of all the extravagances! I was certain that Miss Peake had no intention of going to a party. When I was alone in the schoolroom for a minute, I walked right up to those double nasturtiums and shook my fist at them. Yes, ma'am, that's what I did, and I blamed them for putting those silly ideas into Miss Peake's head.

I could hardly sleep that night trying to figure out whether or not Miss Peake was really going to a party. Next day, I stopped by the school, and going up to her right in front of Doctor Griswold, I said, "Is it true, Miss Peake, that you've bought a party dress?"

She smiled at me, the widest smile I'd ever seen on her face. "Indeed I have, Mr. Tuttle. A gold one with green slippers and green silk stockings to match."

Remember, this was right in front of Doctor Griswold, and I felt my face burn scarlet.

"What's more, I'm going to a party on Saturday night. A very grand party at Vallejo, Mr. Tuttle. A Navy ball! There, how's that?"

"It's all very strange," I said, trying to hide my feelings. "Are you going with an escort, Miss Peake?"

"Perhaps," and she actually was spinning her little gray hat on the end of her pencil.

"Oh!" I didn't stay as long as usual that afternoon, and on the following two days, she had left the schoolhouse before I got there.

On Sunday, Miss Peake and I always saw each other in church, although we never stopped and spoke to each other when we met on the steps. A school teacher with a fine reputation like Miss Peake couldn't make free with men in public places. However, I always tried to sit where I could see her. But the Sunday after the Navy ball, she didn't come to church, so I decided that she must have missed the last trolley from Vallejo to Napa.

It was quite a nightmare, now I look back on it, the change in Miss Peake after that experience. I call it experience, because you never would have believed what a gay time she'd had at the ball, unless you'd heard it from Miss Peake the way I did. In the first place, her gold dress, as she described it, must have looked for all the world like a double nasturtium. Men, as well as women, had admired it more than any other gown at the ball. It wasn't like Miss Peake to speak freely of such things, but she confessed right out that she had even tasted champagne and when she got home there was a big runner in her green silk stockings; that's how she had danced during the evening.

To hear some of the Valley girls, Miss Peake couldn't have had the exciting time she said she had. They wanted to know where she'd suddenly learned to dance. She'd never danced at any Valley party. And how'd she meet this grand naval officer she talked about so much? But to my way of thinking, girls who put red paint all over their mouths can't be depended upon for the truth. They did admit they'd seen the poor old thing start out for Vallejo, all dressed up in her party dress. That's exactly what they called her, "a poor old thing," and I was mad as a hornet.

I tried not to mind, but from the night of the ball there was a real change in Miss Peake, and you didn't have to put your glasses on to see it. In the first place, she began to hum in her class until Doctor Griswold had to speak to her about it. Then she bought a new hat, and would you believe it, right on the front of it was a bunch of red cherries!

I'd always noticed Miss Peake's shoes, which were nice and sensible, but one day I saw her all togged out in high-heeled shoes. "French heels," she said, and I was so dumbfounded, I couldn't speak.

"You aren't going to another party?" I asked her.

"I certainly am, Mr. Tuttle, and another and another!"

Then she walked right out of the room without even stopping to water her nasturtiums. It wouldn't have been so bad if Elmira Fink and some of the other children hadn't noticed her and giggled as if she really was funny.

"My Lord, did you get a slant at old Peake?" That's exactly Elmira's words. "I think she's off for the kill."

That was more than I could stand, and I spoke right out. "Miss Peake wouldn't kill a fly and you know it!"

That Elmira Fink laughed, but I didn't care; they weren't going to talk about a kind-hearted woman like Miss Peake, not with me there to protect her.

But when she came in, the night of the school exercises, with her hair all frizzed out, and the girls flocked around, I felt as weak in my stomach as if I'd eaten those red cherries right off her hat. I couldn't believe my own ears when I heard that Elmira Fink say to her, "What kind of face powder do you use, Miss Peake?"

"Lover's Kiss," said Miss Peake, and all the girls laughed. Miss Peake laughed, too, though I knew she must have been embarrassed.

Her lips seemed a little colored that evening, but I laid it to a fever, for her cheeks looked brighter than usual. I would have given anything in the world if I hadn't looked up just as she raised her hands to pat her hair over her forehead, for her nails were shiny as glass!

"Come on, Miss Peake, 'fess up," said Greta Petersen, who always was too free with the men, "and tell us who was at that last party you went to."

"Oh, nobody much." Miss Peake didn't even resent their impudence.

"Sure there was! Somebody in trousers. It wasn't the naval officer again, was it?"

"Perhaps," Miss Peake said. "Now run along and tend to your own affairs." She was actually laughing as she ran out of the place.

I stopped at the school, next day, to see her, but she must have gone out on the heels of the children. The room seemed so lonesome without her. There stood the nasturtiums dancing in their gold dresses, and I hate to tell it, but I just pushed that flowerpot right off the windowsill and left it lying there broken into a dozen pieces! I couldn't help it. I wanted to get back at her somehow, and I knew that she'd feel pretty bad when she came in the next morning and found it there.

My conscience troubled me though, and I had made up my mind to tell Miss Peake the truth about it, but when I started trying to explain, without making it too personal, she only laughed and said, "Never mind, we'll find another flowerpot, Mr. Tuttle, and the nasturtiums will go on living just as I'm going on living for the first time in my life."

The next hat she bought had a bright green feather on it and if she didn't get herself a coat of the same color! In fact, she began to buy herself so many new clothes that everybody in the Valley grew tired of talking about them. Then Hank Overbaugh let it out that boxes of candy and little presents for Miss Peake were coming through the post office. When he spoke to her about it, she laughed again, with her lips all red, and said, "Would you really like to know? Well, they're from my beau."

To me, it was just as if the Lord had said to one of the two thieves, "Hello, pal, how's tricks?" Something in me cried out, and I couldn't look at Miss Peake again.

I tried to remember her as I first knew her before she bought the gold party dress.

Almost every day a letter came to the post office addressed to her. One day she was so excited, she dropped one. Louie Petersen swears she did it on purpose. Anyway, he picked it up, and you'd have thought it was common property the way he and the other men passed it from hand to hand. I came in just as they were reading it out loud: "I'm dreaming of you day and night, Bertha, and I'll be home soon," the letter ended up.

"It's a real honest-to-God love letter," Elmer Larson shouted. "Well, I'll be damned!"

"Indeed you will be, Elmer Larson!" I told him. "How dare you pry into Miss Peake's life? How dare you read her mail behind her back?"

"Keep your shirt on, Tuttle," he says. "We're all tickled to death to know she's got a fellow. Nothing we'd like better than to see the old girl hitched."

My heart pressed a pain against my ribs the day Miss Peake came to the school wearing a diamond ring on her left hand. "I can't keep the secret any longer, Mr. Tuttle," she said. "I'm going to be married. He's a naval officer, Lieutenant Arthur Pomeroy, and we're to be married when he returns from Panama."

I couldn't seem to find anything to say to Miss Peake after that, but I heard everybody in the Valley talking about all her plans for the future, and they discussed certain things too intimate for me to mention. But a few days before the naval officer was to come, Miss Peake, who hadn't seemed to notice that we had stopped speaking, came over to me as I was painting a windowsill and said, "I'm giving a party for all of my friends on Saturday night, Mr. Tuttle, and I want you to be there."

"But, Miss Peake! You surely don't want *me!*" I was dumbfounded, but she said she meant me to come.

The party was held in the front parlor at Asa Fink's farmhouse, where Miss Peake was boarding. Arthur, that was Miss Peake's naval officer, wrote her to get the finest rooms in the Vallejo Hotel, but as he wanted a quiet wedding so he'd have her all to himself, he told her to invite all of her friends to this farewell party at the Finks' the night before.

The party went on for hours and hours, and everyone had a grand time what with roast pork and roast chicken and fancy dishes for supper, to say nothing of the real wine that Miss Peake said was a present from the naval officer. While the ladies were looking at Miss Peake's wedding things, I peeked through the door. I could see the white wedding gown and the long white veil. But it seemed like I was dreaming and that I'd wake up any minute to find Miss Peake's shiny face looking at me through her gold-rimmed glasses again, or that I'd touch her thin hands as we fussed over the double nasturtiums like we did in the old days.

Sam Bascom brought a sack of rice from his store so we could pelt Miss Peake with it when we left there at two o'clock in the morning!

I'll never forget Miss Peake as she stood in the doorway waving good-bye to us. "When Arthur and I come back from our honeymoon, we'll run over and see you all," she promised, and her voice was pitched so high I thought it was going to break. Before the whole crowd, she leaned over and kissed me good-bye. It was a bold thing for a lady to do. Miss Peake would never have done it before she bought the gold party dress. "Good-bye, dear Mr. Tuttle," she said. "Your friendship has meant a great deal to me, and I wish you all the happiness in the world. And, please, don't forget to water the nasturtiums."

That night, Miss Peake, dressed in her new white wedding dress, long veil and all, went out and drowned herself in Pope Creek.

Some of the Valley folks thought she'd drunk too much of that wine Arthur sent her for the party. Other folks said she'd made up the whole story about Arthur, the naval officer, and had even sent herself the letters and the presents, so they guessed she was a little bit cracked.

I blame it all on the double nasturtiums. But, anyway, she loved them, so I took them out to her grave and left them there for God to take care of.

✤ *from* Confessions of Madame Psyche

Dorothy Bryant

B uddy seemed a mysterious figure, out of place. Clearly he was qualified for a better job than he was doing; most of the attendants had no more education than I. Besides, why wasn't he in the Army, a boy in such radiant good health? I began to notice that other attendants were not friendly toward him. One day when I was wheeled outdoors I passed a group of male and female attendants in the hall (the besetting sin of attendants is to gather in gossipy huddles

From Confessions of Madame Psyche: Memoirs and Letters of Mei-Li Murrow. *Copyright © 1986 by Dorothy Bryant. Reprinted by permission of The Feminist Press at The City University of New York.* Confessions of Madame Psyche *retells the myth of Psyche and Eros through the experiences of a fictitious Eurasian character, Mei-li Morrow. This excerpt is set near the beginning of World War II at the Napa State Hospital, at the time a 2000-acre, self-sufficient farm with a population of 4000–5000 patients. The setting and incidents are based on research and interviews.*

121

until dispersed by an angry charge attendant). I saw that the huddle did not open to include Buddy as he walked by. They ignored him. Only I raised a hand to greet him. It was obvious that their hostility toward him ran very deep.

The mystery was solved on Thanksgiving night when a suicide attempt was brought in, and, doctors and nurses being even more scarce than usual, a call was put out for Buddy. He stopped the blood (she had cut her throat with a razor she could not have gotten hold of, but somehow did) and started a transfusion of plasma donated by the Navy. Then he sat down at the foot of my bed to watch for an hour, to make sure she was out of danger.

We spoke in whispers and in complete darkness so as not to wake the other patients. Perhaps because it was so dark, because he was far from home on Thanksgiving, because he was so tired, or simply because I asked—he told me about himself.

He had been born and raised in Indiana, where his parents were both college professors. He graduated from college at twenty and began medical school. Then came the war and his refusal to go. "I registered as a conscientious objector and was sent to a camp, 'out of sight, out of mind,' just like all of you here. The peace churches are supposed to run the camps, but they just cushion the orders from the military. I hadn't gone through all this just to be hidden away in some boy scout camp, cutting brush! We had meetings, planned actions, had more meetings. How sick I was of meetings! Have you ever tried to explain democratic action to a Mennonite? Meetings broke into factions, and factions of factions. We had classes, a work strike, protests galore. Anything to make waves, to make it impossible to forget us. Some walked out of camp and got sent to federal prison. When I heard we could serve in mental hospitals, I volunteered. Anything to get out to the people, the community, in the world."

He sighed and was silent for a long time. "In the world," he said, in his normal, deep rumbling voice. Then he was silent again for a while before beginning to whisper again. "Another place to hide people, but this one's no boy scout camp. The two boys they sent with me lasted three months. They had to send them back to camp, or they would have had two more patients. I'm not sure how long I'll last or even why I try.

"They keep me on the back wards," he whispered, "with the most withdrawn or violent patients. I got a couple of them tossing a ball last week. Took me all month, but I got them up off the floor, got them washed, into some clothes, and out on the yard. The other attendants say, why bother, they'll just withdraw again. I don't blame the attendants for not caring. The pay is terrible, they get no training, and they've each got seventy or eighty men or more. I'd like to organize them, lead a protest. But I can't, because they won't speak to me." He tried to laugh silently, but I heard the catch in his throat. He was sitting there in the dark, trying not to cry at his isolation, at the terrible things he saw every day. He let me hold his hand for a moment, then stood up, checked his patient once more, and left. I hardly saw him again during the time I was in the infirmary, except when he came to return my book.

The doctor who attended infirmary patients was the admissions doctor, who looked even more pale and worn than when he used to visit his wife on Ward B. I asked him how she was. He shook his head. She had deteriorated further. There was pressure to back-ward her. "She will never leave here if I let them do it." He stopped more frequently at my bed and talked longer than with other patients. At first I thought he wanted the comfort of speaking Greek, but, when I was ready to be released, I learned that he had been observing me with a definite plan.

He wanted to take his wife off Ward B and move her into the house where he lived on the hospital grounds, "south of the hog farm. I need someone to stay with her day and night, watch her, make sure she eats and does no harm to herself, someone who will get her to talk, to walk, to be in the world. Would you consider it?" Consider it? I jumped at it.

The doctor's house was one of dozens scattered among the rolling meadows behind the hospital buildings. Until the war they had all been occupied by members of the staff. Now half of them were empty and deteriorating rapidly. The doctor and his wife had moved into one of the better ones, a three-bedroom cottage behind a knoll from which the hospital buildings were invisible, except for the towers of the castle, whose topmost spires peeked up over the top of the hill.

The doctor moved his things out of the large bedroom and went to sleep in the smallest room. He kept the third bedroom as a study. The large bedroom had a small alcove where a cot was set up for me so that I could be with his wife all night. The room also held a bookshelf and a small desk. There was a small, stiffly-furnished, unused parlor, and a large sunny kitchen, where another inmate did the cooking. Two more inmates came in to clean and keep the garden.

So, after nearly a year on the wards, I entered a life that offered the greatest luxuries: quiet and a little privacy.

My care of Madame Doctor (I addressed her formally with the title and respect she had enjoyed before the war) was simple. At first it consisted of urging her and helping her to get up and dressed and groomed. To eat, to move, to talk. She did not speak for weeks, but I talked constantly, putting in English words where my Greek failed. Sometimes I read aloud. Of course, she understood little English, but I hoped the sound of my voice would be soothing, and would keep calling her to come back, not to sink away from people. She was afraid of darkness, and I could read to myself by the light kept burning all night in our room. Another luxury, the lighting up of evening hours!

I ignored her husband's suggestion that I decorate a Christmas tree for her. I had seen enough of these well-meant observations of holidays on the wards, and was convinced that to a deeply troubled soul they only bring more pain and grief. Instead, I persuaded him to buy a record player. It was Buddy who suggested the music. "Nothing

too cheerful or emotional or romantic. Something orderly, sym-
metrical. I'd suggest Bach, but not the passions."

Buddy had taken over a small cabin nearby where coffins had
been stored in the days before the crematory was built, when inmates
were buried on the grounds. It was little more than a large box, no
heat, no plumbing. But Buddy preferred the coffin house to the angry
stares and slurs of the five regular attendants with whom he had been
sharing a room above the laundry. The doctor liked him, appreciated
his interest in Madame Doctor's health, and invited him to shower
and eat at the house whenever he liked. "I will practice my English in
conversation with an intelligent young man. Hearing civilized conversation will be good for her, too."

Buddy came often. Sometimes he and the doctor argued about
pacifism, but Buddy held his own amazingly well for such a young
man, tracing back all the inhuman steps which had brought us to the
point where the only weapon against Hitler was war. His analysis
reminded me of the events recounted in Stephanie's letters during the
decade before the war, each exasperating equivocation and disgusting
betrayal reviewed clearly by Buddy. "And when these idiots—having
ignored every warning, every suggestion by us 'unrealistic pacifists'
until trapped with their back against the wall—when they say to me,
'now you must fight to the death, kill them all, there is no alternative'—
then I still say, no. We had other choices, other chances. You chose
killing. I choose not to kill. No." In fact, Buddy showed himself so
much better informed about Hitler and all the history leading to
Hitler "than any American I have met; Americans know no history,"
that the doctor almost forgave his refusal to fight, was happiest when
he came home and found Buddy in the kitchen. He did not find him
often enough because sometimes double and triple shifts kept him on
the wards around the clock.

It rained heavily and steadily that January. Even with heavy
boots on, Madame Doctor and I did not go far beyond the garden,
neither of us feeling strong enough for long walks through the mud

or the thick fog that came between rains. But by the end of the month, I was feeling much better, and she had progressed to getting up, washing, and dressing without much urging. Then the rain stopped, and February came.

Of all the many seasons of the California year, February is the most beautiful. Since June the hills have been brown and dry, and the winter rains have only turned them soggy, still dull in the weak sun of the short days. But in February fresh grass sprouts overnight, a bright, iridescent green suddenly flooding the landscape. Fruit trees bloom, the tule fog disappears, and the sun shines as brightly as in summer, without parching the land. The orchards surrounding the hospital grounds resembled those in the Santa Clara Valley, but in the Napa Valley they were mainly apples instead of prunes, alternating with the little, stumpy grape vines. In that blossoming February of 1943, we began our daily walks.

The doctor had given me a pass allowing us to walk anywhere. We turned away from the buildings on the front grounds, discovering and exploring the world behind the castle. On the first day I took Madame Doctor north through the meadows, following the cows on their wanderings out to the fields to graze, then back to the dairy where they were milked twice a day.

On another day we walked south of the main drive (which kept going straight toward the hills after being interrupted by the castle) around the new hog farm. Beyond the hog farm fence, on the east side, stood a high pile of wood, stretching hundreds of feet into the orchard. All the pieces of wood were the same size, rather flat and broad. All were deeply weathered, etched, and marked. We stopped to turn some of them over and examine them. The marks cut into them were numbers. One that I looked at said 1920. Was it a date? Another, on which I could barely read the number 277, was a cracked, rotted old chunk, nearly disintegrated.

The wood pile remained a mystery until we reached the nursery (as close to the castle walls as either of us cared to go), where an old inmate tended seedlings for a variety of plants and trees. He told us that the hog farm was started on the old cemetery, whose wooden markers were numbered by death count. I had seen the markers of inmates in the order in which they had died, bodies unclaimed and unnamed. "Now they cremate, over there behind the slaughterhouse. Can't see it from here. Used to be a big pile of them markers. Mostly used up for firewood."

At that moment the inmate was called away by a frowning attendant whose look showed his strong disapproval of men and women talking together, of women in general. This was definitely male territory. Women worked in the cannery or laundry, but, except for the picking season when all working inmates went to the orchards, outdoor work was reserved for men.

On the days when hogs or chickens were slaughtered or when the crematory smoked, we walked through the northeast orchards. Most inmates with passes went west, down the main drive to the highway, where they might hitch a ride to town. (Local people usually stopped for the easily identifiable inmates.) So we had the backlands largely to ourselves.

Our favorite walk took us back behind the hog farm, past the crematory, and through the first orchard to Lower Lake. Birds nested in the trees surrounding the lake. Under the trees lay thick logs with hollowed-out seats. Here we might sit for two or three hours while Madame Doctor watched the water and the birds, and I read or talked with Buddy, who sometimes brought a group of inmates with fishing lines, proudly pointing to one or two who were beginning to speak again. Lower Lake was a relatively free place, open to all patients, who often brought visitors there. But in the early morning we were alone there, and Buddy would join us when he came off night shift.

Buddy usually started a conversation with a comment about whatever book I was carrying. Often he had already read whatever it was. He had begun reading at the age of three and had never stopped. By fifteen he was reading philosophers I still cannot understand, and historians I find very difficult. He thought nothing of his precocity; all the boys he knew read everything and argued brilliantly, "then went for a brilliant career and didn't read or argue anymore." They all had commissions in the air force now; he never heard from them anymore. His new friends were the men he had met in C.O. camp. He spent his spare time writing letters to them, and sometimes he read their letters aloud to me. He also had a girlfriend who wanted to come to California and work in the hospital with him. "We'd have to marry. What if she got pregnant? Besides, it would be so hard for her. The women are even meaner than the men." I'm sorry to say I could not disagree with him.

His position at the hospital would have been trying even to a more mature man. He was shunned by most of the staff and criticized for being "too easy" with the inmates. He was paid nothing for his work, and though his parents had not repudiated him, they were far away and in poor health, with little money to send him. He was as short of cash as most of the inmates.

Whenever he mentioned a book, I ordered it. I also kept him supplied with writing paper and stamps, insisting that my sister could well afford them. He laughed (knowing a little of my history by then) and accepted gracefully, but he would not let me buy clothes for him. In his off-duty hours he often wore the state-issued gray cotton pants and shirt worn by inmates. This infuriated the other attendants "...because the line between us and the inmates is so thin. The only difference is these." He would jangle his huge ring of keys and laugh again, a deep, rich rumble. "I just thought I'd dramatize our true position for my fellow workers."

The clothes looked comfortable. I asked Buddy to look for some small enough for me. He brought me pants, shirt, socks, all in the uniform gray the inmates hated. From the Navy ward he got a P-coat which kept me warm during early morning walks. I was finally free of the terrible flour-sack dresses and could move more freely on the grounds, mistaken for a male inmate with worker's privileges.

Buddy went on dramatizing reality for everyone. He often ate with the inmates instead of in the attendants' dining room, complaining loudly about the difference in the food. He attended every staff meeting with a list of questions. He wrote letters constantly to the state government, complaining of shortages of food, clothing, medicine, staff, space.

His complaints led to the inspection of the hospital by the governor in 1943. His description of the inspection was hilarious. The director of the hospital was willing to show the worst in hopes of getting more money. The attendants did their best to hide what he exposed, expecting the blame to fall on them. The inmates were frozen with fear of joining either side. And the results? Buddy laughed loudest as he repeated the governor's order to "close the attic immediately," increasing the crowding in the rest of the castle, which the governor ordered "condemned." According to older inmates, said Buddy, he was the third governor to condemn the castle.

What gradually won many of the staff over to Buddy was his humor. Whenever I heard him talking to anyone, I heard his sentences separated by low chuckles or deep laughs. He even laughed at the grisly jokes of the attendants. "People have to laugh," he would say. "These guys care, or they wouldn't have to make up jokes like that." He loved fun. He attended all the Saturday dances, choosing as his partners the oldest inmates, the saddest, the most withdrawn. He did not dance as an act of charity but for the fun of it. He really had a good time, especially if he could make someone else laugh.

Of course, there were times when Buddy's energy and humor deserted him. He would join me at Lower Lake or in the doctor's kitchen, pale and red-eyed, looking ten years older, shrunken, as if his tall, thin body had wasted overnight. Then I would hear his account of some horror like the beating of an inmate by the "goon squad" of attendants called to subdue violent men. He would shiver as I held his hand, and his aged look would collapse into one of helpless, stricken boyhood. Then I would remember how young he was—about the age my daughter would have been. In comforting him, I received the most comfort because during those hours we spent together I was temporarily the only friend he had. Just when I thought my few close friends were lost forever, I had been given a new friend.

Madame Doctor and I took longer walks that summer, making interesting discoveries. There were flocks of sheep in the hills watched over by inmates who rarely came down to the main grounds, but lived in shacks they built for themselves. There were caves where discharged inmates lived like Indian fakirs, unspeaking, sitting draped in rags. In the winter they returned to sleep in the castle basement or in some other niche where they could rest unnoticed. It was rumored that one of the caves was occupied by a woman who provided sex for working inmates in exchange for clothing, food, and other comforts which made her life sumptuous. But I never saw any women in the backlands.

Once we came close to the stone village being created by an old Italian man who carried huge stones up from the old quarry where bricks had been made to build the castle. He had made fences, walks, a tiny house. The smaller stones he threw at anyone who came near. We changed direction when stones began to fly our way, so I never saw him, but I heard him whenever the moon was full. He howled like a coyote.

After several explorations we confined ourselves to the area around Lower Lake. There were too many rattlesnakes in the hills, and a long hike was too risky for me.

I made one other interesting exploration on a day when the doctor had taken his wife to San Francisco for the day. It was a quiet, hot Monday in September. I had walked beyond the hog farm and through the broad stretch of farmland where inmates were harvesting tomatoes and rolling in fruit from the orchards, all headed toward the sheds next to the bustling cannery.

Between two orchards, hidden by a grove of camphor and birch trees, was a long, Spanish-style stucco building: the crematory. It always looked deserted, even when smoke came from its chimney, and no one ever went there, except the worker (not an inmate) who lived there. Now even he was gone, probably to the shipyards, and an undertaker came in from Napa to operate the oven when an inmate died. The front door, through which bodies were wheeled into a refrigerator, then into the oven, was locked, but a little door in the back of the building had been left unlocked.

It opened into the small room where the former employee must have lived. In one corner was a narrow wooden bunk. In the center of the room, taking up most of the space, stood a small wooden table with two chairs. Under a small window was a small sink and shelves. A worn, sweat-smeared felt hat still hung on the wall. Next to it was the door to the bathroom, and in the bathroom, another door, which I opened.

It led into a large, dark, windowless room. Feeling on the sides of the doorway, I pressed a light switch, turning on a weak bulb that hung from a wire in the center of the room, which was even larger than I had thought, at least thirty feet long. All four walls were lined with shelves, from floor to ceiling. Filling the shelves were rows of fruit jars, three deep. I walked closer to the shelves and saw that the jars were labeled, each with a name and a date. The contents of the jars were gritty gray. Each contained the ashes of a dead inmate. There were egg crates on the floor which contained the overflow of jars from the shelves. Most of the crates were full. On the wall next to the door to the bathroom, the crates were stacked to the ceiling. Other full crates were already being stacked against full walls of shelves.

Of all the strange but invariably true rumors which spread through the hospital, I had never heard about this room. Inmates never worked here; some sense of the humane, the decent, kept the attendants from employing them in disposing of their fellows. Perhaps the attendants did not even speak among themselves of this room. Sad as it was, it was an advance over the numbered markers on the old graveyard-hog farm. These remains were at least named and dated, kept for family or friends to claim. That so few were ever claimed was not the fault of the asylum.

❧ from Napa

James Conaway

During the war the price for a ton of grapes rose from $15 to $50. The growers of Napa Valley and the rest of California made money and planted more. Field hands who had made only $1.75 for a nine-hour day now received 40 cents an hour at Inglenook and other wineries—an astronomical wage. And there were not enough workers to be found.

Rafael Rodriguez's father sometimes made kitchen shelves in Mexico City from wood salvaged from fruit crates. As a child Rafael had dismantled the crates and had often paused to look at the labels on them showing, in vibrant colors, orchards, lush fields, and hazy mountains in a northern land called California.

Mexico languished in an ongoing depression during the years of the Second World War. The 1910 revolution in Mexico had failed. An ocean of deprivation and cultural heritage still separated rich and poor. Rafael was keenly aware of the difference between the people and the authorities, those well-dressed figures glimpsed in the Zócalo outside the presidential palace. Common men still had to remove their hats when approaching these people; sometimes they knelt and muttered, "In God's name."

His father was an *obregón,* a worker in a textile factory. He was often unemployed. The Rodriguezes lived among the capital's *vecindades*, slum tenements of the barrios of Tepito. Later Oscar Lewis would describe Tepito in *Children of Sanchez* as "a poor area with a few small factories and warehouses, public baths, run-down third class movie theaters, over-crowded schools, saloons, *pulquerias*....This area ranks high in the incidence of homicide, drunkenness and delinquency."

Rafael's father had been part of the mass migration to the capital from the countryside. More than a million and a half impoverished people lived in Mexico City in the early 1940s—a third of the population. Though illiterate, he managed to marry into a family of merchants. Rafael never knew his mother, or even her name, and assumed she died in childbirth. Her mother cared for Rafael as a small child, and he remembered the sweet, musty odor of green bananas smoked in a room off the courtyard, to age them before they were sold.

His father, a handsome man with a mustache and unmistakable Indian features, often came to the house, only to be turned away. "He's a street vendor," Rafael's grandmother would tell Rafael.

His father came and took Rafael away when he was five. His father was jailed for this but eventually Rafael went to live with him, his second wife, and their children in the small house in the barrio. His father belonged to the Confederación Regional Obrero Mexicana, but the textile mill ran intermittently, and then not at all. The family existed by selling clothes from a stall in La Merced, the big market, or on the street. Then Rafael and his father would cross Mexico City on foot, pushing a cart loaded with clothes bought cheaply, including handkerchiefs made by Rafael's stepmother. They sold them to buy beans and tortillas cooked in lard on the roadside.

Rafael's stepmother made soup from tiny fish bought in the market. There was no plumbing in the house; Rafael and his step-brothers had to walk six blocks to fetch a jar of water. Often there was not enough to eat. Mexico City was in turmoil, with more people arriving daily without money or the prospect of jobs; competition in the markets was fierce. Rafael knew how to read and write, and his father, using union connections, managed to enroll him in technical school when Rafael was thirteen. There he learned to operate the big looms, but he found little or no work.

He had heard of El Norte. He didn't know exactly what it was, only that it lay far north of Mexico City and that there a man could earn more in six months than in five years in Mexico. He also heard that El Norte was the exploiter; he saw thousands of poor people in line outside the Estadio Nacional, fighting to join the braceros. The braceros were promised jobs in El Norte. Rafael couldn't believe their determination. They stood and slept in the lines, peddlers sold them food, and others rented them the use of buckets so they could relieve themselves without losing their place in line.

Rafael told his father about this possibility of work and his father said, "If you have to go, be good to the Americano, and he will be good to you."

Rafael was so hungry he ate banana skins off the floor of La Merced. One morning outside the Estadio Nacional, he stepped into the line of braceros. Within hours he was surrounded by people from the provinces—Indios—who spoke a strange Spanish. The man in front of him asked Rafael if he had worked in the fields. Rafael said no, and the man gave him a piece of lead and told him to rub his palms with it, to build up the calluses and to add color to a city boy's hands.

The second day the door opened and hundreds flooded into the building, Rafael among them. There they found more lines and food in boxes. Each man was given two pieces of bread with a slice of meat, a piece of pie, and an apple. A huge gringo in a khaki uniform, speaking broken Spanish, asked Rafael's name, where he was from, and what farm work he had done. By then Rafael knew the answers the gringos wanted: he had planted rice, he said, in Guanajuato.

The gringo examined his hands and sent him to another line. A gringo told the men to undress. They looked at one another and then complied, and marched into another room carrying their clothes. There gringos in white coats subjected them to degrading examinations, x-rayed and photographed them, and told them to return the following day.

Rafael heard his name called. He was handed an envelope. Inside was a card with a photograph of a slight, dark-haired young man looking confused, a number—61353—and words in Americano, stipulating that he was to earn no less than 37 cents an hour.

He took the card home and showed it to his father, and the next morning went to the train station with a blanket. He and hundreds of other men boarded old railroad cars that had been fitted with rows of straight-back wooden seats. It was February and there was no heat on the train, and no food other than tortillas and frijoles brought by the lucky ones. Rafael did not know where he was going or how long he would be gone.

Rumors spread that the braceros were sold into slavery, that they would never see Mexico or their families again. The crowd on the railroad siding shouted, *"No vayas! Bajate!"* Don't go! jump!

The train lurched northward.

Food ran out the second day. For diversion, the men sang, accompanied by a guitar in the hands of a bracero from the state of Hidalgo:

"Yo soy como el chile verde llorona,
Picante pero sabroso."
 I am like a green pepper,
Very hot but very good.

Rafael trembled with the cold; he was exhausted. The train stopped once at a remote siding outside Durango, where he could see nothing but fields of grain, and took another day to reach the border. There the men sat for three hours before the door was opened and they were ordered across the tracks—into Los Estados Unidos. Rafael sniffed the clean air.

A passenger train waited, shades drawn; inside there were padded seats. Gringos told the braceros where to sit and not to raise the shades. Masses of food appeared on paper plates.

Early the next morning Rafael took a chance and pulled the window shade aside; he saw desert and dry, distant mountains. The rumor was that if the train turned right, they would end up in Chicago. If it turned left, they were bound for California. So far the train had not turned at all. It entered a vast plain of houses and eventually pulled into a cavernous station, where they were allowed out onto the platform. This, he heard, was Los Angeles, but he couldn't be sure. The gringos waved them back into the train and all night they sped north.

At dawn the train stopped in the middle of a flat landscape. Furrows ran off toward infinity. The men left the train and lined up in the bright sunlight. A Mexican woman told them in Spanish that they were not in Chicago but in Watsonville, California, and that they would pick lettuce for a large company in Salinas. A bus took them to the bunkhouse in the Watsonville barrio, known as El Paharo. There were outhouses, a communal shower, and food not as good as that on the train: frijoles, pig's feet, flour tortillas.

At four the next morning they were fed mush called oatmeal, and then packed into buses that took them thirty miles through the dark to the still-frigid fields. There Rafael learned to use the cortito, a small hoe for thinning lettuce. The work was hard and the day very hot, and the men arrived back at the bunkhouse after dark, dirty and exhausted.

At the end of two weeks he was given not money but a slip of paper with his name and wages written on it. Rafael didn't know what to make of this. At the store he was told to sign his name on the back of the slip of paper and then was handed $75. In Mexico, it would have taken him two months to earn the same amount of money. Seven and a half dollars had been taken out of his pay and sent to the Mexican government; he had the feeling that he and the other men were being rented to the gringos.

Most of the other men were illiterate. Rafael helped them sign their checks. He and a friend he had made on the train were still city boys; despite the real calluses on their hands they felt out of place, trapped in the bunkhouse, the bus, the endless rows of lettuce. His only outside contact was the Mexican woman, an American citizen who worked for a government agency known as the Food Administration. She saw that Rafael and his friend were different and one Sunday invited them to dinner. They showered, put on their best clothes, and waited outside the bunkhouse until she picked them up.

Her mother's house was the first American home Rafael saw; to him it was luxurious, and the food incredibly abundant. Here were good Mexicans, he thought, who had accepted El Norte and apparently been accepted by it.

A young Mexican American working for the Food Administration was assigned to an office in a place called St. Helena; he asked Rafael and his friend if they wanted to go with him. On impulse they packed their clothes and left.

Passing through San Francisco, Rafael looked up at the white buildings, steep hills, and blue bay. Girls on the street wore shorts, something he had never seen. The car crossed a great bridge, where fog poured in from the sea. The sun came out again, and they crossed lowlands and headed north through a rich agricultural valley. Rafael had forgotten about the rural scenes on the fruit box labels back in Mexico City. Looking out at plum orchards and rows of strange vines running off at perfect angles from the highway, he was reminded of those visions.

In St. Helena they were met by a taciturn man named Charlie Wagner. Without ceremony he told them to get into the back of his pickup and then drove wildly through the dust and potholes to a ranch near the Napa River. There was a vegetable garden and chickens. To Rafael's surprise, Wagner gave each of the young men a Coca-Cola and then introduced them to his wife. She took them out to the shed where they were to live. The beds had been made. That night, at age twenty-two, Rafael lay down between sheets for the first time.

If hoeing lettuce in Salinas had been exhausting, picking plums—what the gringos called prunes—was crippling. Much of the time Rafael spent on his hands and knees. The crew was paid by weight, and the others were used to the work and impatient with the newcomers. Rafael also had to shake prunes loose from the trees by placing a pole against the branches and throwing his weight against it. If the prunes didn't fall immediately, a dozen people screamed at him.

His knees bled and his hands blistered. He cried at night. Wagner turned out to be a kind and fair man—the first real farmer Rafael had ever met. He told Rafael and his friend they would have to find some other work; they didn't have the stamina for prunes.

Rafael went to a nurseryman in Napa named Salvator Emmolo, an Italian who spoke broken Spanish. In Emmolo's nursery were grape vines. They appeared to be dead, but Emmolo taught him how to cut the long canes so new ones would grow in the spring. The canes were piled at the ends of the rows, collected, and burned. All that January smoke rose over the valley, pearl-gray columns against the green mountains and blue sky.

Emmolo taught Rafael to graft new vines onto old rootstock and then to wrap them to assure that the buds survived. The work was not physically hard but demanded concentration, and Rafael found that he liked it. Emmolo was patient. He even put Rafael on the tractor. He had never driven one before and had not been allowed even to approach the tractors in Watsonville. But Rafael knew how to operate the machines in the textile factories at home, and he learned to run this farming machine. The fact that Emmolo let him try raised Rafael's opinion of himself.

Some others in the valley were not kind. When Rafael went to a store the owner did not want him to touch things he didn't intend to buy. There were many places he could not enter, and girls he could not look at.

He married a Mexican who had become a U.S. citizen, but Rafael had to return to Mexico, as required by law. He left his wife and an infant son behind. Then a change in immigration law gave him the opportunity to return. He went back to work in Napa picking tomatoes, prunes, and walnuts, and gardening. Wineries were few and far between, and what went on in them remained a mystery to Rafael.

One day Emmolo took him to Rutherford and introduced him to a big Portuguese named Sousa. He was the foreman of a vast ranch and vineyard known as Inglenook, with hundreds of acres of vines and a towering stone winery that was the finest thing Rafael had seen in Napa. Mexicans were not allowed to work in the vineyards except to pick up cuttings and to weed and cut brush. Pruning was left to men of Italian and Portuguese descent. Sousa would pay him $1.25 an hour, which seemed like gold to Rafael.

When Sousa discovered that Rafael could drive a tractor, he let him move with his wife and now two young children into the little house between the winery and the Victorian mansion owned by the Daniels.

Sousa taught him how to drive the big D4 Caterpillar and sent him to the cellar when wine needed to be racked or moved. At those times Rafael came under the direction of the winemaker, George Deuer, the rudest man Rafael had ever worked for. He shouted and cursed at those he didn't like, and seemed maniacally jealous of his position. He recorded dates, grape tonnages, and other figures in a notebook he kept in his desk drawer. He didn't want others looking at the notebook, and if Rafael or anyone else entered Deuer's office when he wasn't there, he became enraged. But from Deuer, Rafael learned the rudiments of winemaking.

First he punched down the thick crust of grape skins and pips that collected on the top of fermenting wine in the huge redwood casks. Walking along the overhead beams, carrying the wooden punch, he felt intoxicated from the smell of the gas put off by the fermenting grapes. The wine drained through hoses down to settling tanks on the first floor. From there it was pumped into 2,000-gallon upright oak and redwood casks at the south end, beyond the Captain's Room and the sales office. Rafael shoveled the heavy residue of fermentation, known as pomace, out of the presses and onto a primitive conveyor belt. From the winery the pomace was trucked to the fields and vineyards and spread as fertilizer.

He picked grapes during harvest, in the mornings. Rafael and other Mexicans lifted the grape boxes one at a time and dumped them over the side of the crusher—heavy work for small men. Then Deuer would come out of the winery and shout at the men to stop. The winemaker simply couldn't handle any more fruit with Inglenook's antiquated equipment. One small crusher served the entire winery. Sometimes the electric pump would be overwhelmed by the volume of wine, and Deuer would emerge again from the shadows, shouting, "You damn Mexicans!"

Sousa allowed Rafael to do more than menial work; he taught him to prune, even though the other Portuguese workers were jealous. Rafael learned to distinguish among the twenty-two different grape varieties at Inglenook. The vines, which had always seemed strange to him, took on new life.

Rafael's wife had a weak heart. She died unexpectedly and the children went to live with Rafael's mother-in-law. Rafael was still a young man; he didn't fully comprehend what had happened, or that there might again be an element of happiness in his life. He devoted himself to work and found comfort in the huge, drafty, mostly empty winery, with its gravel floor—cool in summer, clammy in winter— and its powerful, pungent aromas. Rafael scrubbed and painted, and once climbed to the top of the peeling cupola, from which he could see the fields of Cabernet, the railroad station at Rutherford, and the mountains beyond.

from To See the Dream

Jessamyn West

Friday

I shouldn't write one word here this morning. Journalizing, like reading, should be the sweet which comes after the meat and potatoes, not before. But this morning I'm having the sweet first. This is the most beautiful, beautiful morning of wind. Of all the phenomena of weather, wind is to me—I started to say "the most moving" but there is a pun in that and I'm too serious about the wind to permit any levity in speaking of it. I have no idea why this should be so; why, if I hear a strong wind coming up, my heart swells with a prophet's pleasure on hearing God's voice speak out of the whirlwind. In fact, I am such a wind-lover, the voice of the whirlwind itself is enough to transport me. (Pun, again, alas!) When I was a child, I often went out to our barn for the pleasure of hearing the wind blow through its cracks. I would sit there on a sack of rolled barley and listen to that ancient, everlasting, and universal voice. Someone commenting upon the inordinate joy Thoreau took in the sound of the wind blowing through telegraph wires put it down to his lack of opportunity to hear music. Poor Thoreau, the gist of this comment was, having to substitute the sound of wind whistling through telegraph wires for Mozart and Beethoven. That writer may have understood music, but he didn't know a thing about the wind—or Thoreau. The wind is no substitute for music, any more than the sea is a substitute for Debussy's *La Mer.*

If I had not lived as a child in a place where the wind blew perhaps I would not have learned to love it so. Or to love it so much, anyway. For I am afraid that one of our limitations as human beings is our inability as we grow up to increase our lovingness by increasing the number of things to which we respond. So I may be a wind-lover by the chance of living in Yorba Linda as a child, where every afternoon one could hear and feel the wind that came inland off the sea, and experience on less frequent and more exciting occasions the glory of being buffeted by the great dusty Santa Ana which roared in off the desert through the San Gorogino Pass, scaring orange groves and filling the airy bungalows with layers of sand. I have always loved the names of the great winds of the world and have collected and cherished them as other women collect cups or lusterware. Monsoon, williwaw, mistral, simoom, chinook....Recently, reading Guy Murchie's *The Song of the Sky,* I had the most—maternal, I think, is the word—pleasure in finding the Santa Ana, the much-loved wind of my girlhood, listed among the great winds of the world. I smiled with all the fondness of a mother who sees by the papers that her daughter has been elected homecoming queen. Local wind makes good! My Santa Ana listed and defined. For the Santa Ana, I discovered, is a "down wind," very treacherous, a wind that has caused more air accidents than any other. I never knew in my girlhood that the Santa

Ana was a "down wind," a wind falling off mountain heights into valleys; but I did know, when the green-gray dust cloud, which presaged its coming, rose like a pillar sixty miles away, anticipations of great joy. Ranchers and housewives hated the Santa Ana. But its coming was a lark for children—or it made children larks. We fashioned sails, kitelike of paper, or shiplike of cloth, and abandoned ourselves to its power; and if we were not lofted like birds we were at least winged and wind-propelled.

This Napa wind is nothing like as strong or exciting as Santa Ana. In the first place it has a dull name. It is called "north wind," a sure sign that no one has loved it or feared it. Perhaps, if I live here long enough and love this wind enough, I can get it renamed. It comes after rain: the air clears and in February seems to take into solution some of the greenness of the grassy earth. In the night after such a clearing, I dream of the ocean. I hear the beat of heavy surf along a shallow beach; I hear crested waves draining back without violence to deep water. But sometime in the night I waken and recognize the surf sound for what it is and smile and think, wind tomorrow! For the first audible sign of the coming wind is this ocean imitation in a long double row of ancient eucalyptus trees a quarter of a mile from here.

The single most beautiful tree I have ever seen in my life is a eucalyptus on the road between here and St. Helena. Most beautiful because in addition to the grandeur of its size and the perfection of its shape (a real tree-shaped tree if ever I saw one) it is subtly colored, in shades that range from the bone white of its massive trunk through all possible variations of greens and grays and blues. And here and there is a flame-colored leaf burning like a candle in the depths of the green-gray gothic nave. I haven't much Druid blood in my veins, but if I were to worship trees, I know the one I'd kneel to.

Poems, in spite of the fact that only God can make a tree, have given me more pleasure than trees. I think, though I pray I may never have to make the decision, that if I were required to choose whether the trees of the world or the poetry of the world should disappear, I would say, "Good-bye trees." A poet, after all, can bring trees into being in his poems. But no tree has ever written a poem.

I might love trees more if we didn't have so many about our house—big-limbed, thick-leaved valley oaks which dispute the sun and the stars with me. Unlike Eastern people who, I understand, greet the first swelling buds of spring with pleasure, I sometimes shake my fist at the big oaks when I see them preparing to open once again their dense green umbrellas. I think sun is better than shade, stars better than leaves, and blue skies better than green canopies. Try to tell an oak that, though! It will laugh a green leaf right in your face.

Individual trees, however, I do revere. I know an acacia which carries more that is glittering than the Mother Lode and does it in a better place. Slanting over a stream so all of its mirrored gold is multiplied by two—and even when it parts with its load of blossoms, it gilds the stream beneath once again. Eucalyptus—acacia. These are not natives of California but came to us from Australia and New Zealand—and I never see nor smell acacia without remembering what the tree is called there—mimosa—and that mimosa was Katherine Mansfield's favorite scent. It is easy to understand why. Katherine Mansfield, ill for so long, hated the cold and suffered from it—and loved the sun and warmth; and if there is any scent under heaven which is heavy with warmth and colored by sunshine it is the mimosa. It is best to smell it *in* sunshine, as all good things are even better when the circumstances are toward. But I don't know any other scent, unless it is that of red roses, that will so lighten gray skies and warm icy airs.

There is a madroña which I can see at this minute standing on the bank of one of the two streams that circle the hill on which this house is built. It, like the eucalyptus, sheds its old bark each year to reveal trunk and limbs as satiny-smooth and cinnamon-shining as those of the Indians who gave Napa its name. In fact its contours and colors are so human that, in long days of rain, I am concerned for its drenching and wish I could ask it in to dry. This is the truth, and it proves, I hope, that I am no undiscriminating tree hater. I only hate *some* trees, as even dog-lovers admit to feeling some dogs pestiferous. If I traveled around the country as Oliver Wendell Holmes, Senior, did, in a horse-pulled gig, I would be a tree-lover of his kind. He loved individual trees and knew the vital statistics of the notable ones in his neighborhood in the same way today's connoisseurs know the vital statistics of movie stars—and he learned those statistics in the same way: through measurement.

So, a tree is to measure, as a hole is to dig. And it is also like the cracks in the barn, to make a wind sound like God's trumpet—or his oboe or his flute. Or all of them together in a full-dress orchestration. John Muir could tell by sound alone through what kind of tree a wind was blowing. I can't do that, but I think I could never mistake, in whatever part of the world I should hear it, the sound of the wind in a tall eucalyptus.

These enormous oaks, which appear in calm weather rigid and unmovable as rocks, are switching about now like buggy whips. I don't know what sounds they make. Occasionally there is a lull in the eucalyptus roar and then I think I hear the unmusical horse-fiddle scrapings of the oaks. But if no treat for the ears, the oaks are now a sight for the eyes. Dr. Johnson did not appreciate an act simply because it was rare or difficult—women preaching, dogs walking on their hind legs. But part of my pleasure in the present sinuosity of these oaks is accounted for by the difficulty. How do they do it? How *can* they do it? Pepys—and my mother—were of a different breed from Johnson. Pepys said he was always with child with curiosity to see any new thing. And Mama too. I am halfway between Dr. Johnson on one hand and Mama and Pepys on the other. I will not go very *far* to see a new thing, but if it appears outside my windows I won't scorn it because it's unusual. And I will admit that the sight of oak limbs flexible as kittens' tails is more interesting to me than willows similarly supple. And if a willow wants my attention, let it become sturdy. Thus do we conspire to see nothing truly, but only objects out of character.

This is the time of the year when I hate the oaks least. Now, except for a few live-oaks, they are leafless. At evening they crosshatch, but do not shut out the sunset. Its light blazes through the interstices green and gold and apricot. In the morning through these openings I watch the spur of a faraway hill change from blue to purple to rose. It is my alarm clock by color. Rose means: get up. Perhaps, like the rest of the contrary world, I would not value these revelations if I had them scot-free, season in and season out with no need to outwit leaves to win them. No pleasure without defiance. I hope this is not true of me; the fact that I hope probably proves that it is.

The Duck Pond At Mini's Pasture, A Dozen Years Later

Philip Dow

Walking out, I flushed some meadowlarks—
Now they're down, and redwings gone into cattails.
A loose strand of barbwire begins softly thrumming.
Out over San Pablo Bay, clouds
Blow up from sunset, fading yellow
Off the Indian Tobacco.

Remembering all those nightfalls
Spent anywhere rain gathered
In corn or barley fields and ducks flew,

I hunch in pickleweed, shooting distance
From the pond, make a raspberry
With my lips and roll a whistle for Greenwing Teal
The old way learned from my brother.

Mosquitoes rise out of sedge. White faces
Of Herefords bob dreamily as they graze.
In quirky teal-like flight, bats
Startle. Oil slickens my thumb on the safety
And I rub it into the marred walnut stock
Of the Winchester double, sniffing
Hoppe's lubricant, souring weeds in the flooded pond.
Behind me, darkness comes on.
A shitepoke crosses the Evening Star.

Far off, beyond the eucalyptus groves,
A pair of mallards
Cross the powerlines—
And I call, rough-voiced. They weave, dip,
Then flare. Afraid they'll pass,
I call again and my throat burns. They circle,
But I don't turn. I know to watch over water.

Out of darkness overhead, drake first,
Slowly they drop, rocking gently
On set wings, down
Slowly, into the last light—

Twilight In California

For My Father

Day of hunting done,
you find this downhill climb hardest.
But where the vineyard road begins
you balk. Breathing the good scent of sweat
and gun oil, you sit cross-legged and tense,
your hunting cap brim full of grapes;
the valley cupped below, shadowless—
waiting for the wine to be poured.
First darkness sifts out of trees into your hair.

Beyond the last ridge
your Rockies pile up,
enfolding wings, antlers,
hides of slain game
that rise, now, in twilight,
with spaniels, moving down gametrails
to drink.

At day's end
your blue eyes rust
like buckshot, changing
wine to blood.

One Verse of a Song

M.F.K. Fisher

It is too soon to write the real story of the house I lived in for a long time in northern California. The Judith Clancy drawing shows more of its western Victorian dignity than I can, and its strength and beauty, and the honesty of birds in trees and tolerant cats dozing beneath.

When my two young girls and I bought the house, in about 1954, it lay under a passing cloud of sadness and decay. I went into the long dim kitchen once, and at the end of a big table sat a skeleton of an old woman, staring remotely at trays and platters and plates of rotting food that neighbors had brought to her for countless unheeded days.

Books of philosophy and early feminist writings were tumbled on shelves and piled in corners on the floor. Over the sorrow and the stench, I felt the vitality of her and of her house, and I was by nature unafraid of ghosts.

Before long she was snoozing off in a kind cousin's warm, clean sheets, and my girls and I were scraping and painting and airing her fine old house.

Below the high first floor there was a half-underground basement that ran the full length of the building, as was the custom in Napa Valley when many of its settlers were Italians who wanted to store their wines and olive oils and grains in dark, cool places. The floor was partly paved, with little runners in it for the rainy seasons, and the thick foundations, about forty inches high, were of local stone, often dry-laid by the Chinese laborers, a dime a dozen in St. Helena in 1870 (or more correctly, about sixty cents for a twelve-hour day). The workmen laid clumsy cement tops on their stubby walls, which later made fine shelves for our plates and books.

After the house was aired and brightened according to our tastes, and a few ghosts made their peace with us, we invited some Boy Scouts and 4-H buddies to dig out the half of the basement that had been left walled but unpaved. Vague legends were used as bait: the old doctor who had built the place, a miserly eccentric, was said to have buried treasures under trees and in heaps of rubble...

The young people worked like stevedores, bolstered by healthy snacks and swigs and dreams of hidden gold, and they did dig up some artifacts that pleased me, no matter how disappointing they may have been to the diggers. There was a Chinese paring knife, with a teakwood handle inlaid in pewter and a strong, pure blade of steel. It sharpens well, and I use it almost daily. There was also a crude but lovely rice bowl. And there was a tall six-sided bottle of brown glass, with a tiny neck. The budding medicos and farmers who uncovered it assured us, with discreet titillation, that it had probably once held a specimen fetus, coming as it did from the old doctor's leavings, and

I never asked them how much more than a cobweb could have passed through that opening. I still have the jar, a handsome thing on a high shelf.

In the basement we installed several windows, short and wide, of what was then called cathedral glass, almost the color of the bottle. The rest of the dirt floor was paved, always with the artfully graded little runners for possible flooding in the rainy seasons, because we were below the gravity-flow level. We put in a half-bath. Part of the space turned into a kind of wine-cellar pub, and there were beds for four people, like couches, in other stony places. We put thick hemp mats on the floors, and hung a few translucent bamboo screens between some of the beams that held up the whole house, and there were books everywhere on the wonderful wide ledges.

The big stone base for the fireplace upstairs stood in the pub, a handsome wall of stonework more probably laid by an Italian mason than by the Chinese. And there was the hulk of the old gas furnace, with five ugly asbestos arms taking heat to the first floor. It was infallible, never-failing, ready to take over at the slightest drop in temperature and quiescent as a happy dog in the hot dry months, so that the basement itself stayed warm or cool as needed—a magic trick!

Much of our time, during the years we lived in St. Helena, was spent down there. It was fine for good bashes and dinner parties and meetings. It was easy to bring edibles down from the kitchen, and the wine was already there! And soon after we moved into the house I found myself working more and more in the basement, so that finally everything I was pondering on was down there, close beside the bed I grew to prefer to all others in the lighter rooms upstairs.

The main floor had two bedrooms for my children. Now and then, as they gradually left for schools and as we all gravitated into the basement for various reasons connected with peace and its components, the girls gave their rooms to the people who sometimes came to stay with us. Now and then I myself would sleep in one of them, for a change or if the runners were gurgling after a storm. But up in the attic was my official bedroom, even after I sank permanently into the basement.

Like it, the attic ran the whole length and width of the house. The roof sloped sharply to the eaves, of course, but there was plenty of fine stand-up room down the middle. The front part was partitioned with heavy chicken wire from the rest of the generous space, and people told us that this may have been to contain some relatives of the dotty old lady from whom we had bought the house. We knew better: her sons had once raised pigeons there, to fly in and out the tiny lamp window, and we had cleaned out a lot of feathery old dung, certainly not human.

At the other end of the attic, looking west, the handy sons had built a fine room over the back porch below, with a whole wall of windows and plenty of room for my big bed and many bookcases, and a few old trunks and cases set against the redwood walls. It was a good nest for my nightlife, until with the force of time and gravity I sank more and more into the dim quiet depths of the basement. I always went up there, though, to be alone when I needed to.

In between those two levels, on the first floor, the house was airy, filled with clear colors and the lacy flicker of light through bamboo leaves. The woodwork everywhere was flat white, and the floors were of large black and white tiles (vinyl, but more than adequate). The ceilings were all fifteen feet high. The walls in the front room were "museum gray," fine for pictures and long bookcases and old rugs, and there was an excellent, if rather ugly, brick fireplace at the far end as one entered from the little hallway. The front door, with a dark yellow glass panel in it, had a funny handbell built in, with a loud mean ring. It was really a good room.

The kitchen behind it was good too, and almost as big. The walls were dark green; the furniture was brown; everything else was white. It matched a copy of one of my favorite *Braques* above one of the two long bookcases, opposite the kitchen counter and across from the generous table, which often seated ten at a pinch, or preferably six or eight.

Off the two main rooms were the children's, with a bath and a toilet where the plumbing was old-fashioned but adequate. And to the left of the front door was a small office (doubtless where the doctor had pulled teeth and set bones and so on), which after my short happy tenure there with my typewriter became the glory hole. Extra copies of books, wrapping supplies, Christmas decorations, picture frames too bulky to carry up the narrow stairs to the attic, boxes that might someday be useful—they all went into this family reservoir, which by some miracle kept its own chaotic tidiness.

Plainly, it is hard to know which room in the house was the best, the most pleasing, but perhaps it was the back porch, under my attic nest. It too had been built by the handy boys who'd kept pigeons, and the many windows and the seams in the flimsy walls jammed and leaked and bulged now and then, but we forgave everything for the bright welcome that seemed to spread out from it the minute anyone came up the narrow steep back stairs and inside, no matter for the first or the hundredth time. Its long row of windows looked out into a giant fig tree. The walls were a light clear yellow. The curtains were of a soft red plaid, and the linings of all the open supply shelves and china cupboards were of the same red. The floor was black and white, of course. There were two good old rocking chairs. We kept table linens in a big highboy. There were racks for fruits and vegetables. The place was reassuring.

People grew used to the fact that the outside house would look shaggy and shabby while we lived there, and they came to feel easy within it. Outside, it was a soft faded mustard color, half-hidden by carefully controlled masses of Peking bamboo. Inside, it was a charmed mixture of light and color, where the air was always sweet and the leaves made fine delicate curtains against the wavery old glass in the tall windows. The fire drew well on the hearth, in winter. In summer, the basement was a cool, dim, windless cavern.

Other people now take care of the Dear Old Lady, as a lot of us call her, and they have made her look tidier than we ever did, certainly. She will outlive us all. Of that I am sure. And as long as I can, I'll sing my own songs of love and thanksgiving for the lives she helped us lead.

—Glen Ellen, California, 1980

The Hot Look of July

After the sun went down it grew cool and sweet, and across the little valley I watched, as I do almost every night, the darkening high ridge of desolate craggy mountains between me and the ocean, and then the nearer somewhat greener hills of a county park with easy trails for junior citizens and those in the "golden years," as our local brochures say to anyone who looks at them.

It felt fine to be in this world again, and not waiting for it to come around, as it seems essential to do for those two or three hours of near nirvana in the late afternoons. We lie naked and spread-eagled on our sheets, inertly waiting to come back.

Across the valley, an ugly, bright hard light comes on after the sun sets, and I did not realize until tonight that it is set to ward off prowlers who might rightly surmise that the hillside property is largely vacant, owned by rich occasional tenants. I always try to block out this light as I watch indolently, peacefully, from my balcony chair. I look instead at a familiar, the big owl who sits for a long time on my one tall pole in the meadow and then suddenly is not the top part of the pole but a great silent dreadful swoop of wings and the end of a little mole or mouse in the sloping meadow below. It is a time for carelessness, and I may hear a small cry as the hawk at the top of a dead tree down in the meadow swoops for another creature and lifts him up in his lethal claws. But there is a general air of watchful surcease.

Tonight, though, there was too much activity along the highway that runs down on the other side of the meadows, under the first low range of hills that make the park. The park has two entrances, one into the grounds and one into a higher-up place that is occasionally lit at night with one big yard globe, as if somebody might come in later. The globe is further up and to the right of the ugly light.

Tonight, as the sky faded from a fine, clear hot sunset into cool darkness, I saw that the ugly bright light had been set so that it went off at perhaps five-minute intervals, and that when it came on, after that lovely nonlight, it was at first a small bluish glow that turned within perhaps two minutes into the lean cruel white light I had come to avoid. It would go off, then glow into brightness again.

As I watched, a car came down the park road and slowly turned right, to the south as often happens, but this time I noticed that before it eased into the patchy weekend traffic, it blinked its lights twice.

Then a car that passed it coming south blinked its "far" lights, and after the first car got out onto the highway, the second car turned around and headed north.

At the mouth of the other driveway down from the ridge of low hills, a car that had come down without any lights, from the house that sometimes burned the ugly bright light all night, suddenly put on its high beam, so that its lights streamed across the highway and up into our meadow just as the car that had turned around passed it. That car blinked twice and went on. The car from up the hill kept its lights on as if it were waiting to come out carefully onto the highway. Finally it turned off its lights completely.

By now dark had almost come. I sat on the balcony feeling a little like the owl on the telephone pole, the hawk on the branch, waiting.

After perhaps two minutes, the darkened car flashed on its lights as if it had just come down the highway, and turned south and went on out of sight, but as it passed, the old light up on the hill that had been going off and on at planned intervals for at least an hour suddenly flashed out strongly three times: Eeee-Eeee-Eeee. The car blinked its headlights once, and disappeared.

I waited, but everything looked as it always did from my balcony on a hot July night. The new moon was almost down, and a jet plane lowered itself gently toward the city, coming perhaps from very far away. A few cars went up and down the old highway. I thought that maybe tomorrow I would hear on the early radio news that a big drug bust had been pulled off, or that child abuse rings were rampant again, or that maybe in twenty more minutes we would not have much more time because some current Strangelove was loose, pushing buttons.

A supper of cold salmon and blueberries with cream tasted fine, if you care about those things, and I'll sleep well, except that I wonder if heat has anything to do with people giving each other signals with their yard lights and car lights. I doubt that there will be any news tomorrow about this.

—Glen Ellen, California, 1980

The Old Cherry Tree

Hildegarde Flanner

Together with a few human beings, dead and living, and their achievements, trees are what I most love and revere. In my life and my concerns I have defended trees that are threatened and praised them when they are ignored; for their sakes I have made enemies of friends and neighbors. The knowledge that in a western canyon I am the owner of very tall straight redwoods and firs gives me pride of citizenship beyond anything I might accomplish by my own efforts. I have taken a serious kind of joy and a delightful kind of peace in their shade, and at night I have watched the shaggy, white planets pass above their dark branches. I have loved trees; I have planted trees, and have been excited to grow a tree from seed and discover the first minute sign of unfolding life that will, some distant year, become a rooted tower or a spreading bower of rustling foliage. I am fortunate to live where native trees are numerous and where horticulture is popular and every rural family has an orchard.

Our own orchard is old and contains many trees that are dilapidated, but even the most dilapidated have been safe for years because each time I look at them, aware of their crookedness and awkward appearance, I also see some odd curve of bough or improvisation of flowering that make sudden poetry of them and of their trashiness. They are thus protected, although they should, under good management, be sensibly discarded and replaced. Yet the more dubious they look, the more they resemble the paintings of Oriental masters and suggest the fresh enduring emotions of the ancient anthologies. Perhaps there is universal truth in implying that real meaning is wrung out at the last moment, and the last moment must be prolonged. Whose duty is that? Really not mine. Yet I have discerned it. I am involved in its total meaning, of tree and of human. Still, as I myself grow older and, alas, much older, the image of new young trees in place of the old ones creeps temptingly into my mind. It is a troubling image and its disturbance, just now, settles on the spirit of a woman wandering and trying to think in an old orchard.

If I could have the sense and courage to take down a decrepit tree in spite of its fanatical habit of reminding me of the brave words of General Su Wu written down 2,000 years ago as he sadly embraced his wife for the last time, and in spite of its mad annual impulse to bloom and bear and spill bushels of amethyst prunes and rosy apples on the ground, it might be for me a spiritual rejuvenation and consequently even a beneficial thing for the flesh as well. But conscience is tyrannical. It is a womanly vice. I have become the guardian not of my own but of whatever other life remains in the earth I possess. It is hard to be wise and natural. Although my husband is no longer living I can guess what he might wish to do. To remove a tree that had lasted too long and replace it might well please him. This thought is a poignant incentive, also a consolation for the choice I foresee as melancholy and difficult, whenever it must be made.

The decision I am afraid of, on a mild February morning of our western spring, is one for advice from a clinical priest. It is beyond horticulture. It becomes moral. In my mind it faces and fights itself and I am torn. Must I continue to identify myself with the aged, no longer serviceable, and eccentric trees, or do I dare to relate myself to young trees with futures, good looks, and green chances of tonic sap? My orchard, by usual standards, is conspicuously shabby. This hurts me. And as I look around I notice a few unrewarding cherry trees.

To get a cherry in our orchard has meant to rise early, before birds or worms are awake, and snatch at a fruit or two as day breaks. One summer, in order to enjoy the large, luscious black Bings, my husband ordered a nylon net he saw advertised in an agricultural supply magazine. The advertisement promised protection to fruit from marauding birds and complete accessibility for the picker. If all of this was true, we were not the ones to demonstrate it. As we hoisted the net on poles to the top of the tree the clinging mesh snagged on every twig on the way up; then, as we squinted into the sun and gave helpful and confusing suggestions to each other on how to free the net to slide down as directed, we found that it could descend only by being profanely and scrupulously removed from twig to clutching twig. However, the picture as given of happy people congratulating each other outside the net while the cherries waxed abnormally big and the birds fretted on the next tree—in the advertisement they were scowling—this fine fiction was worth keeping in mind until suddenly and utterly we tied ourselves in. The next step was just to ripen along with the cherries in boredom and frustration, while the birds jeered nastily. This very personal recollection comes back to me as I find myself standing under a cherry tree, not the one that lassoed us, but a very old pie-cherry tree, largest and surely the oldest inhabitant of the orchard. Indeed, where is there in the entire valley a cherry tree so old and so big? It is a tree known in the neighborhood, and when we first came here to live friendly strangers drove up our hill and requested, "Just a few cherries, please, from the old tree, enough for the wife to make one pie."

Now so much of the tree is fallen or dead that there is scarcely enough fruit for a robin to make one cherry tart. I get none myself, even on tiptoe or a ladder. And the trifle of birdsong it holds is nothing to give regard to. Neither has it grown ancient with picturesque aspects. All of its gifts are gone. Even the child with a little basket passes by. It is too large, you see, to be forgotten, yet neglect is its fate today. And so I talk to myself as I look up and see no buds swelling toward wide-open blossoms where the bees should soon be rolling. From something so unpromising, what is to be expected? Why is it so difficult for me to say, "It is time, old cherry tree"?

This happens to be the day on which my son is preparing a level space where there will be built a storehouse for tools and equipment. I welcome this plan as one to maintain order. Not only his powerful tractor, but various archaic automobiles considered by him too beautiful and valuable to go to the dump, can now be respectably housed, particularly that very sacred hot-chili-red truck that usurps the sight of grace and elegance where my tallest bamboo has established its feather culms. This is a day of orchard and premises keeping, and its purposes begin to take hold of me. I look up at the cherry and assess what I see. Crippled and lumpy, here and there split, beheaded of several heads, and to all appearances, so nearly dead that there seems no way to say it is alive. Then I look up at the sky and straighten, as if to think of other things. A good clear morning to be alive myself. And John has opened the deer gate and is driving the loud clanging tractor into the orchard toward the work that makes ready for his storehouse.

"Oh, John," I call. He doesn't hear above the roar of the machine. Without thinking I reach out and touch the subject I was about to speak of. I touch not only a tree of bark and wood, but with tingling certainty in my fingers, I touch an entire century. At this spot there stood a house which no longer exists. The spring that served its occupants still serves us from its cold stone trough at the edge of the nearby woods. And a county clerk had written the first deed to this property, dated 1878, in script almost too lace-like to read or believe. It was then that the tree was planted and began to work for men and birds, and until this spring it has never stopped working. It was always the first to bloom and ripen, always prompt no matter that the weather might delay, still it brought on its sweet sparkling globes of fruit. For 100 years of faithfulness there should be a reward. Hang the old tree with garlands, strike up the fiddle. But I am caught up in another momentum. Again I call, "Oh, John!" He can't hear, there is too much noise. I go closer. "Maybe it's time," I shout, and he yells, "What is it?" How hard it is now for me to be positive and loud, quick and wise. But I must not take time to be careful. I am committed. "Time to take down the old cherry tree," I shriek.

I know that decisions like this should be made in quietness and deliberately. We should live slowly, even timidly, in imagination with all the possible results of the irrevocable. Once down, there would never be an up to this deed. I exercise a frightening power. It is not exactly a choice between life and death because life is already attacked by mean and obvious details of the end. However, the power of termination is awesome. Naturally, it chokes me. I cough. Kings, tyrants, judges—how have they arrived at that last fatal word that condemns life without feeling their own lives threatened, shredded, and about to come apart? But don't be silly, I say to myself. What are you talking about? Just get on with what there is to do. Isn't this the mistake you have always been making? Too much emphasis on the wrong thing while you let the right thing drift? "John!" I shriek again. "Time to take down the old cherry tree!"

"Yes, yes," he says easily, "I can hear you," and I become aware that he has turned off the noise of the tractor and also that in the interval of silence I can hear the demented sound of the ranging peacock that forages in the foothills and ravines near our place. It always seems to be a sound of mental stress, and at this moment it is right for my state of mind.

I am surprised by hesitation on John's part. "I don't think I can cut it down, it's too big," he says. "I'll have to push it down." Again he seems doubtful. "If I can."

And the tractor starts again. Then for a while he is busy with his work of leveling nearby, but as I stand watching he begins to look at the old cherry tree in a calculating way. I suspect that he welcomes my decision to get rid of a tree so dominant yet unproductive in this place, and he must be astonished. He circles and comes closer. I cringe and brace myself for the shock to my nerves and my conscience. John backs his tractor and then goes forward with an awful clang. He hits the old cherry with a loud, dull crash. It does not budge. It does not even quiver. He backs away. Again he charges forward and collides with the tree. It stands without shaking. It is only I who grow weak. I shake and feel sick. Perhaps I am wrong to condemn a creature so full of strength in spite of the many signs of being done with strength. Again the tractor charges and without effect. I would prefer to leave now, to go back to the house and hide behind closed doors where I could neither see nor hear; but it was I who started this turmoil, and I must remain to see it through.

At this moment my thirteen-year-old grandson, Danny, arrives and stands near me, watching. "Your father is wasting a lot of good gas," I scream. "Diesel," he screams in return. "Fuel," I scream back at him, as the attack continues. Backing and charging, backing and colliding, the tractor roars and hits, and at last the old cherry tree begins to tremble. But it stands. I suffer and watch in a nauseating agony of indecision. Should I save the body while some secret obstinacy still holds it up? Or is it better to let the savage shocks continue? Suddenly John begins a new maneuver. He backs, then closes into the attack at an angle, tilts the sharp, wide blade of the tractor, and digs it into the earth. Again he does this, and again, until the action of the bellowing machine and the chaos and the frightful uproar become a kind of violent choreography. I stand riveted and overcome by what I have started in the quiet orchard. Finally the tilted blade snags on a massive root. The root holds.

The contest goes on. My son will not give up. The old tree will not give up. The tractor will not give up. The boy and I stand and wait, and the diabolic ballet goes on and on. The tractor, although a monolith, has been converted into a maniac of circling and twisting power. In its fierceness it is serpentine. At last, at last! With a heavy snap, a sound of fatal resignation, the root breaks. And the tree still stands! The tractor attacks it for the final time. And when the old cherry tree falls there goes down with it a century of hopes and many kinds of weather, sun and drought, of good rain and poor rain, of good pies and poor pies, and 100 years of countless round, white flowers opening and coming apart and drifting down while early-rising and late-loitering birds and bees came and went and always, at the right cloistered moment there was the invisible sap slowly storming up through the trunk and into the tips of the branches, just as it was rising in a million other trees at the eternal hour given for ascension.

While I stand and have no voice to speak John nonchalantly gets down from his tractor and walks over to the fallen tree. He begins to peel off patches of thick bark. "Termites," he says. I do not want to see them. "More termites," he announces. I hate the sight of them. I stay where I am. Then he pulls off another, larger patch of bark. "Look here!" he cries. There is a company of small lizards, eight in all, spending the winter in the shelter of the cherry tree. John collects them and quickly puts them all down Danny's back. The boy rolls his eyes and draws up his shoulders but does not flinch.

I retrieve the young saurians and put them in the grass. Then I go to the prostrate tree to hunt for more, as if this intimacy with small creatures might reduce the magnitude of the old giant's final resignation. There seem to be no more lizards, but I find neat necklaces of empty holes, the precise work of woodpeckers whose echoing labors I have often heard. Then John, in the cavity left nearby, finds a beautiful little snake of a dark rich skin, a young gopher snake whose presence close to the tree appears to indicate dependence and community. John holds the snake for a moment, and we watch as it flashes its rapid tongue in the sunlight. Then he puts it down, and we see it take off, small and solitary. We are left alone with the fallen tree. It is stripped of everything, except its misshapen size and its weighty bulk so lately upright and adamant. There it lies.

John gets his power-saw and starts methodically cutting branches for firewood. So soon does the drama and ordeal of destruction become the routine of plain use. Dazedly I pick up a few small logs. "Are you out of wood at your house?" he inquires.

"No," I answer, "This is ritual. I want a few pieces of the old cherry for my bedroom fireplace."

He tells me, "It won't burn yet. It has too much sap."

"Too much sap!" I exclaim and hastily drop the wood. "Is it still alive?"

"Well, what do you think? You saw how the old girl fought back."

His personification of the old tree horrifies me, and I begin to cry.

John gives me a well-controlled look. "You're queer," he comments.

With difficulty I inquire, "What's the diameter?"

"Three feet at least, I guess. Big for an orchard tree." And he goes to work again.

In wretchedness I pick up the pieces of wood and hug them, small logs of smooth bark ornamented with delicate silver-green medallions of lichen. I carry them ashamedly to my bedroom porch. When I lay them down I know that I will never burn them, ever, no matter how long I keep them to lose their sap. They are too elegant, they have too much meaning. I shall never wish to warm myself at their melancholy and accusing blaze.

I return to the orchard. It is a still, empty place now. John has driven his tractor back through the deer gate, and Danny has gone with him. I stand and stare at the remains of the old cherry, the limbs in a heap, thick bark strewn, the powerful roots split and twisted. Now no one else will know if I give in to tears as I realize that there must always be new questions in my mind about the imperfection of my decision to remove the old tree. I have learned, too late, that there is more to life than what is visible. The greater strength had been underground and out of sight, and I had grossly, stupidly, not even guessed it was there. You fool, you made a wrong choice, and you only proved that decisions are hell, a fact you've known since tormented childhood when it was not possible to be sure whether vanilla or strawberry or chocolate was the right choice, or whether to wear the sash with rosebuds woven into the silk or the blue satin one or the one with Roman stripes. I observe how tough the roots are and how strong and sharp and that they point up with a kind of spiraling hiss into the placid noon sky. How dreadfully eloquent they look, expressing all that I felt for them. It is not easy to stand alone with them.

Something prods me into an attempt to understand that the moment holds a finality beyond agitation. In weariness I can only decide that an urban-minded person would take this with helpful sanity, and I shall never be an urban-minded person. "For you they pulled out oak, fir, madrone, and manzanita," I say to the roots. "It was a long time ago. Do you remember?"

For many minutes I stand here where the first axe wound and the first gouge of the plowshare cut into this very ground at my feet where the old cherry tree has just been knocked over. Now I hear the tractor again. It is down in the vineyard. "All right," I say, "It's true that I am queer. I talk to trees. I talk to roots. It's true they can't answer. But they have a lot to say. Look at them!" And I myself look at the roots where they lie on top of their trash, full of fierce power in every slashed point that thrusts up, full of a cherry tree voice, full of a forest voice, the forest that fell to make room for an orchard 100 years ago.

I start back to the house. "Just to get out of earshot," I tell myself.

✖ Winter Blues

Kate Braverman

T here is the sound of rain, there is always the sound of rain. It is a Thursday in January in the Northern California town of Cotati in what will be a year of record-breaking cold and floods. It will be the year of Chernobyl. She will always remember the day the nuclear fallout passed over her condominium complex, how thunder was sudden, how a kind of blue ice fell for perhaps fifteen minutes. It was singular, how blue the air became. The news that night didn't mention it.

Erica watched her daughter make snowballs. It was such an astonishment, this cold blue anomaly, that Erica did not think it might be dangerous. One tarnished cell producing a string of pinheads, like a

From Squandering the Blue. *Copyright © 1989, 1990 by Kate Braverman. Published by Fawcett Columbine. Reprinted by permission of the author.*

cool tracer bullet through a thousand generations. That did not occur to her then, only later. But now even Chernobyl is months away.

Erica has a paper due in her modern American poetry class. If she can complete this paper on time, she has only one more semester of course work before her teaching credential program. For reasons no one has adequately explained to her, there are vacancies in the fifth grade. She could expect immediate employment.

Erica is trying to type while Flora sits on her lap, while Flora crawls over her and pulls the electric cord from the wall and crumples the pages as she types them. In between, Flora demands pudding. Then she needs macaroni and orange juice. Flora asks for crackers with jam on them. She requires one napkin after another. Erica has learned to make sandwiches and sponge up spilled milk while simultaneously rereading lined-in yellow-crayon passages from a textbook. She has learned to give the appearance of being physically present when in fact she is somewhere else entirely. Or perhaps this is a kind of emotional sleight of hand she always knew. Perhaps it is a rare intrinsic gift, something she was born with.

Now she is attempting to explore the issue of why so many American poets have destroyed themselves and what that tells us about our society. She has chosen Hart Crane, Anne Sexton, and Sylvia Plath as examples. In between she must mix flour and water into a paste for Flora to make collages, for Flora to stick photographs cut from magazines onto sheets of gray construction paper. In between she must change her daughter's clothing, locate sweaters, then a second and third pair of knee socks. She must brush her daughter's hair and teeth.

Erica is thinking about Hart Crane jumping off a ship near Cuba. Suddenly she wants to fall to her knees and pray for the poets. She imagines them with immaculate ravaged faces, with necklaces of ransacked moons, with teeth which are black stubs. Poets are collections of unused crescents and bandages, confused images and terrible departings. They wear poisoned cameos. There is the prophecy of bridges and remote trains.

Flora is pulling the sleeve of her sweater. Flora is asking her to change Barbie doll clothing. Erica struggles to guide the doll arm into the miniature garment. Then Flora asks for ice cream. Erica tells her to get it for herself.

"I can't reach that high," Flora explains. She is patient.

"Get a chair," Erica screams. "Use two hands."

She is always telling Flora to use two hands. It is possible that symmetry is not natural. It is somehow an acquired trait.

"I can't," Flora admits. "I just can't." She looks startled and frightened. She begins to cry.

Erica sighs. It is later, after the ice cream. Erica is drinking Russian vodka straight. She often thinks that the only way she will stop doing this is if someone captures her and somehow sews her mouth shut. Four months later, when she hears that the nuclear reactor at Chernobyl has melted down, her immediate reaction is to drive through Cotati buying bottles of Russian vodka. Just in case the Russian water supply or air becomes so contaminated it affects liquor exports. Just in case they stop making it.

It is eight P.M. The rain has stopped or perhaps, and more likely, merely entered a brief period of remission. And what does the flagrant self-destruction of American poets tell us about the quality of our lives? This is what Erica is thinking as she arranges Flora in front of the television set. She places a white cotton pillow beneath her daughter's head. She surrounds Flora with her favorite stuffed animals, her panda with the velvet paws, her large gray raccoon, and her shaggy white dog with the heart-shaped name tag on a red plastic leash. Flora orders more toys. Erica goes upstairs to collect them. There is the pink bunny that makes music when you shake it, the white-and-black cat with the mouse that sticks to its paws, the drum from Disneyland, crayons and coloring books.

The television is a permanent static at the periphery. It is the new perimeter of her sensibility, a kind of fence or lower register that seems sharp and metallic. She carries her vodka bottle to the window. There is the smear of rain and the abscess of night beyond it. Erica is thinking that poets know there is nothing to see in the sealed sky. The moon is black as a gutter dog. The sky is a kind of zoo. There are no celestial matings.

It is too cold to sleep in their bedrooms upstairs. Flora and Erica have been sleeping together on the living-room floor in front of the fireplace. They lie down with their clothing on in a sleeping bag. Flora falls asleep quickly. Erica listens to the rain. She remembers the city of her birth, Los Angeles, and how she could hear the city breathing. It was some sort of organic ruin, an accident of architecture and brutal necessity. There was an inspired pulse beneath the shell. The iridescence was somehow almost legible, suggesting a calligraphy of exposed bone, transparencies, experimental skin grafts. The blood of Los Angeles was a red neon wash, a kind of sea of autistic traffic lights. In the mockery of stillness, the insistent repetition would clarify itself. It was the sound of transition, not an absence but a seizure of competing postures and rituals. There was abundance where there should be none. It was a form of diversity so distorted and rapid that the sudden mutations were actually audible.

Now there is the density of this other northern night that remembers rivers and forests and rain. Perhaps this night has compassion, this night that is of the elements, the untarnished imperatives of this earth. She considers poets with their heads in ovens, with carbon monoxide hoses in their mouths. It is some final act of alchemy, perhaps, the transmutation of gas and poison into a substance that absolves. There are small blue flames on the kitchen stove. Such blue things anchor worlds. It is always a poet's winter. They stand with their feet at the edge of night bridges. Their toes reach over into the great blue nothing. The world stalls and holds its breath. We are children again. We know the cool blue definitions as a child knows not to cross the road or touch flame. Then we touch it.

It's been weeks without sunlight. Morning is a damp gray, as if there had been a monumental transgression that required an unexpected punishment. She considers the gray of London in 1963. It was raining when Sylvia Plath committed suicide. Perhaps the air was dangerous and wounded. It felt cold and soiled. Plath had shed the world as it actually was. She had penetrated into the inviolate chamber, where the mystery was ceaselessly unraveling across the illusion of cool blue glass. And in the manicured parks, only violets and lilacs and asters. All the colors of bruises, violence, and disaster.

Cartoons begin in eight minutes. If she can keep Flora occupied that long, she will be able to sit at her typewriter and consider aspects of self-destruction in the lives of modern American poets, how they have engineered the particles and made the ruinous aesthetic. You could breathe the gas in and it would be a series of individual blue jewels. Suicide would be a kind of clarity, a turquoise definition. It would be like falling in love.

Slabs of granite glow red and explode. The air is torn. Men with deformed faces threaten little girls who wear rings that paralyze and sting. There are hints of incest and perversion. The rules of gravity have been suspended. This is the apocalypse of childhood we carry with us and never forget. Cartoons have begun.

"I'm bored," Flora tells her again. It is later. Flora is pulling on the left side of her sweater.

It was the coldest winter in decades, in England, in 1963. Sylvia Plath had discovered the subtle equation between elements, the slow tidepools and follies of morning. The way there is no north or south. And now there is nothing left for her daughter. They have exhausted the forms of diversion. They haven't left the apartment in more than a week.

"I'm bored here," Flora screams, pulling the typewriter cord from the socket. Her daughter's fists are clenched.

Okay, Erica concedes, leaning against the kitchen wall, pulling on her boots. Okay. We'll go outside. Then she is buttoning Flora's navy blue raincoat and leading her through puddles to the carport. Then she is driving through swollen streets wondering where a woman alone with a child can go in a rainstorm. A woman without a single friend in the county on a January day when a record rainfall will occur.

She is driving north on Petaluma Hill Road. Later, in May, the countryside will be startling with wild yellow flowers advancing to the horizon. Later there will be a soft green wash across the rolling hillsides with their cows, their acres of pasture and sheep. Now the road is a bare suggestion between a gray without seams.

She will take Flora to the Santa Rosa Mall, she decides. The mall is an enclosed area where they can walk and remain dry. The assault of listless color will amuse her daughter. Erica parks in the underground structure and notes that this particular mall is orange brick. It is a kind of morgue for the not yet dead. Flora begins humming.

The mall seems almost deserted. The barrage of oddly muted neon and garish window displays is somehow halfhearted. They are selling a style of clothing Erica wore before her daughter was born. She allows Flora to run into a toy store. She sits on a bench, smoking a cigarette and listening to rain collide with the roof.

She realizes that she has been wearing the same clothing for days. It's been too cold to change. Her nightgown is a kind of permanent inner layer she tucks into her jeans. And it suddenly occurs to her that she has spent the last four years in one shopping mall or another, on interminable afternoons and weekends, in rain and on holidays. She is always a woman alone with a child in an alien landscape. A woman who does not know a single person in the county.

There was a mall in Maui, in Kahului, near the airport. She would go there after her slow morning walks along the ocean and before the ritual of sunset, when the sky was pagan corals opened and surrendering in a mime of sexual abandon. That was when the sky was the pink of irradiated flamingos and fuchsias. She would drive from the apartment she rented in Lahaina, across the eight-mile strip of ruined sugarcane to the jungle side of the island, to the mall. She could wander unmolested there. When her daughter became tired, she carried Flora in her arms.

Derek wasn't living with them. He was staying in a shack without electricity in the jungle. He was becoming a pot farmer near Hana. He came to see them in Lahaina at Christmas. He was lying on the sofa watching football on television. Then he was screaming that he couldn't stand it.

She carried her vodka glass into the hallway. The glass had become almost part of her body, like another appendage. It seemed organic and effortless. Derek was in the bathroom, his eyes narrow with rage. "I can't use a flush toilet," he said. "I've lived outside so long I get cramps if I don't squat." He was staring at her as if this was somehow her fault. She was always compromising him. She blanched at international borders. She trembled when customs agents opened her suitcases. Now there was the matter of the child. Derek kicked the door and the wood split.

Then it was late afternoon in the Kahului Mall. Flora spent hours staring at parrots and hamsters. Her daughter's capacity for the pet shop was limitless. Their afternoons were informed by canaries and puppies, turtles and goldfish. Flora remained indifferent to landscapes, to the intoxicated air, the way the skies seemed lava, primal and unsubtle. Flora was perfunctory in response to waterfalls, macadamia groves, cliffs of ti plants, and stalks of torch ginger. Flora did not care if they lived inside a postcard. Flora was watching a kitten sleep.

The Kahului Mall was a kind of DMZ. Here she was simply a nameless shopper without history or resonance. She was an anonymous woman with a child who had somehow come to the islands and would go. She was merely a woman holding a net shopping bag, glancing at the price tags on aloha print dresses. She was camouflaged and inviolate. She smoked on the bench outside the pet shop. The pet shop smelled of grit and mystery and childhood. The fish tanks were dark and cool and seemed vast, the way a movie theater did on a Saturday when she was seven. Now Erica carried a soda bottle filled with vodka. She accepted a card for a free lei-making class, for a series of hula lessons. Derek was in the jungle and he wasn't coming back.

Erica walks into the toy store in the Santa Rosa Mall. It is two years later. Flora wants more Barbie doll dresses, evening gowns, bridal ensembles, and cocktail party skirts. She has selected a Barbie office outfit with a tailored jacket and knee-high red boots. She also wants an expensive mock medical kit with a clever toy stethoscope inside, a plastic thermometer, realistic eye chart, and rubber syringe. Erica agrees to buy it.

They are home in the early afternoon. There is no way to fill up this day. She turns on cartoons for her daughter. She thinks of the wine country she has just driven through, how the weight of it feels like a violation. She has never been graceful with transitions.

Her husband, Derek, had an ease with borders. With him she knew it was all simply a matter of color and angles, of love affairs begun and ended at airports. They had portable identities. She carried several passports in her purse, mosquito repellent, cash, a Swiss army knife, and a paper fan. There was no terrain that could surprise.

Erica considers Derek and the hotel rooms that lie between them. Always a shuttered window is opening onto an alley or a plaza with a monument, bronze soldiers school children leave tulips for. There are mountains beyond the city. It is India or France or Peru. Derek has removed the cameras from his neck, the many eyes he thinks justify him. He has fallen across a sofa as if harpooned. He will remain that way indefinitely. In between she will make herself smell expensive. She will put on lipstick, kohl, and high heels. She will put on pearls and a silk scarf at her neck. She will visit doctors and collect codeine prescriptions for him.

Derek will not tour the museum or take her to dinner. Beyond the hotel window, up a hill, are the ruins of a city Homer mentioned. Derek is watching "Hawaii Five-O" on television. It is dubbed in a language he does not speak. He studies the edges of frames, searching for something familiar. He is transfixed, as if he expected to encounter old friends.

She is watching him. She is always at the edge, too, watching him. She is drinking vodka and pain pills. Derek would be gone for months in the desert or mountains or jungle. Then he would send for her. He would watch television relentlessly. There would be constant room service. This was his concept of the civilization he rejected. Always, he was turning their hotel rooms into convalescent homes. He is immobile on clean sheets, trays collect. When he is stronger, he will order newspapers and magazines. He is lying in one bed or another like an invalid.

She can remember the smell of his flesh. It seemed coated with a fine dust, some residue from alleys in villages 8,000 years old. And market stalls and bells from churches, a sense of music escaping from the mosques. There are sails on one blue horizon or another and piers with the sound of wind in tin. Always there are the fishing nets pulled in after dusk. And she thinks of Maui, with the ocean blue beyond blue, livid, newly formed. It was on the other side of the lanai. It needed neither purpose nor justification. It was a blue beyond the postcards. The sea and jungle resisted reproduction. The actual colors were an extravagance beyond the camera. Hawaii could not make itself small and conventional enough for the lens. Nothing could accommodate the glare of the plumeria. Or the green in all its permutations, uninhibited, rebellious, startling. And the ocean, with its ruthless and implacable incaution. After a time, Derek stopped taking photographs.

Flora asks her to switch television stations. Then she wants her to change Barbie doll dresses. She insists that Erica find missing doll garments, that she coordinate dresses with the appropriate shoes.

Erica considers throwing Barbie against the wall, or yanking out her arms, or biting through the neck. She could sever the head of that icon of anorexia. Instead, Erica opens the new medical kit, the one Flora begged her for and now doesn't want to play with. Erica touches the stethoscope and then the rubber syringe.

"Barbie needs a fix," Erica says. "Help her out."

"Is that a joke?" Flora stares at her. She places her hands on her hips.

"Yes." Erica is drinking vodka and smoking a cigarette. It is still afternoon. It is still raining.

"It's not funny," Flora decides. She turns her back on her mother and slowly walks away.

Erica sits at her typewriter, considering Sylvia Plath in London in winter. And Anne Sexton in Boston. They also had daughters. They must have worn their nightgowns all day. Or perhaps they wore their other lives like cotton frocks in a pastel simultaneity. Then they forgot the calla lilies, the Sunday church bells, the afternoons of white moths and lies that clarified and defined them like a perfect translation.

Later Flora wants to be a princess. Erica must adjust veils and devise a method of attaching lace curtains to her daughter's shoulder. She must create a train that is dramatic and functional. It is still raining. It is after dinner. Erica carries the vodka bottle with her from room to room.

They have been sleeping in front of the fireplace for warmth. Now they are out of wood. Erica carries her daughter upstairs to her bedroom. She puts a fresh red sweater on her daughter. She brushes Flora's teeth and hair. She places her daughter in bed. Then she closes the closet door against the possibility of demons and ghosts. She reaches down and turns on the night-light, an ornate bulb surrounded by cowrie shells. Derek bought it for Flora one August afternoon in

Lahania. Now Erica has given Flora the seven magic kisses for under her pillow. She imparts the seven magic kisses on each cheek.

"You forgot my brain kiss," Flora informs her.

Erica was standing near the door. She returns, sits on her daughter's bed, kisses her forehead. I'm not going to get through this, she thinks.

"What about my foot kisses?" Flora is staring at her.

Erica extracts her daughter's legs one at a time. She kisses the soles of her feet. Erica has already placed a glass of apple juice on the table beside her bed. She has already rubbed her daughter's back until the dark brown eyes began to close. Flora has already said her prayers.

"I want a bedtime story," Flora reveals. "Tell me about you and Daddy and the rats."

Erica takes a breath. "The rats in Nepal? In Katmandu?" she asks. "We used to feed them twice a day, like cats. We just put food out on a plate for them. We had rats in India, too. There was typhoid. We were a twelve-day hike from the doctor. Not a real doctor. A missionary who might have some training."

"Tell me about the mosquito nets." Flora is smiling.

"Daddy didn't believe in them, not even in East Africa. He said anything that bit him would die from the toxins," Erica says.

"I want to hear about the gun." Flora says, her voice soft.

"You remember that story?"

Flora laughs. "Yes."

"It was a fishing village in the south of Spain. We rented a car. I was driving," Erica says, squinting as if she can see it better that way. "Daddy was too sick to drive. We heard there were Peace Corps people in the mountains. That was the rumor. We got there and they knew next to nothing about the poppy trade."

"They were vegetarians," Flora tells her.

"Yes. You remember everything. And they had no idea which doctors in Valencia would write prescriptions or which pharmacies would fill them."

"Then what?" Flora closes her eyes.

"Daddy took out a pistol and pointed it at them. 'If I find there's smack around you haven't told me about, I'll come back and kill you,' he said. Then he pointed the gun at me and said, 'Is it true?' I said, 'Believe him.'"

"Daddy really wanted that smack," Flora says.

"Yes." It is still raining.

"What's smack?" Flora asks.

Erica considers the possibilities. "It's a kind of poison," she says.

Is it possible that it is raining even harder? It is a permanent damp night. In Spain, twenty years ago, Derek was too sick to drive. Later that evening, she put on a silk suit and pearls. She told the doctor at the emergency hospital that she was a tourist with a bad back. She had left her pills in Paris. Then she was smiling, gracefully opening a leather wallet and removing cash.

"Is Daddy coming back?" Flora asks.

The wind is howling. They are out of firewood. And she is a long way from the tropics, from the particular corrupt heat that nourished her. There is nothing on the other side of the window but the cold, dull night and the moon who moans in all dialects and forgets nothing.

If it continues to storm, she won't even be able to drive Flora to the Santa Rosa Mall. She has heard on the radio that Highway 101 is closed in both directions, that the alternative roads have washed away. Bridges across the Russian River are gone. People are stranded in the hills. She remembers how she looked today, reflected in a shop mirror how long and gray her hair is, how strange she looks, with a nightgown stuffed into her jeans, with a flannel shirt and wool sweater and down jacket on.

She remembers Derek in her apartment in Lahaina. It is the day before she left Maui. Derek is banging on the door.

He is ringing the bell and yelling. It is not yet dawn. He is kicking the door. He has a knife in his hand.

"Cut me," he says when she opens the door. He indicates a spot on his leg.

Erica stares at his leg. She looks at the knife. "I beg your pardon?"

"Cut me." Derek is insistent. He points at his leg. "You can do it. Cut me enough so I go to the hospital. If I need stitches, they'll give me codeine."

Flora has woken up. Erica holds their daughter. She looks into her husband's eyes. It is a door into a corridor she no longer wishes to enter.

"Cut yourself," she decided. "Cut your throat."

"Is Daddy coming back?" Flora repeats.

She says, "No."

Erica stands in the living room. Then she sits by the fireplace which is filled with yesterday's ashes. Erica cannot imagine any mechanism by which this winter will ever end, this rain and this night and its exquisitely venomous sisters.

It is winter in Los Angeles, in the city of her birth. The moon there is full, tranquil, and undamaged. In Los Angeles she had a house on a hillside. There were pale butterflies in the backyard above bougainvillea and freshly risen stalks of bamboo. The night was vivid with a fascination of purple jasmine, kisses and lamps and the ambiguous scent of amber. The abstract avenues were informed by the small coherence of jacaranda rising like twin columns on both sides of the street, erasing the concept of leaving or arriving.

It is four or five months from Chernobyl and the blue rain that will deposit its strange ice in her yard, the day the fallout the authorities called harmless passed above Sonoma county. The day the sky ached. The next morning she will drive through Cotati buying Russian vodka, just in case. It is less than a year from the October when she will, quite by accident, attend a meeting of Alcoholics Anonymous and get sober.

Now there is a kind of snap and the lights go out. The electricity will remain down for six days. She is out of firewood. She sits alone in the dark.

Erica thinks about the lives of American poets in this century. They leap from bridges and ships. It is an elongated January of derelict inventions, of perpetual mourning and amulets. The poets put their heads in ovens. They are drawn to the pulse of the blue flame. Their skulls are plazas of grief and rotting. They have depots and piers inside their eyes. There is the terrible heartbreak of going. Then they put the carbon monoxide in their mouths. Always they are sick beneath a devious scripture of moon. It is a season of crimes. They are wearing their diseases like garlands, necklaces of plumeria. They walk in circles in shopping malls. They are searching for something ineluctable and they are never certain. Then they leave their children orphans.

The only light in the house is the match that lights her cigarette. And it occurs to her that the only light in the world is the flame that is killing us.

from Assembling California

John McPhee

The Napa Valley is thirty-five miles due west of Davis—
an easy run for a field trip, a third of it flat and straight.
The occasions have been several, not to mention spontaneous, when
Moores and I have made westering traverses, collecting roadside
samples of rock and wine.

After the level miles of field crops and fruit trees and almond
groves, the ground suddenly and steeply rises in oak-woodland hills,
so brown and dry for much of the year that geologists working among
them can accidentally start fires with sparks from their hammers.
Putah Creek, the stream that has spread its fine silts to Davis, is here a
kind of door to the Coast Ranges, spilling forth their contents,

coarsely bedded. Among the stream's cutbank gravels are layers of air-fall tuff that descended from the coast-range volcanoes of the Pliocene, and conglomerates that contain serpentine pebbles, peridotite pebbles, chert pebbles, graywacke pebbles, volcanic pebbles—the amassed detritus of several geologies, suggesting the commotion in the rock to come. Also present are fine-grained remnants of extremely fluid basalts that burst out in the northwest in middle Miocene time, covered areas the size of Iceland in a single day, and are thought to have been the beginnings of the geophysical hot spot that has since migrated to Yellowstone. The Columbia River flood basalts, as they are known, reached their southern extremity here.

As we go up the stream valley and arrive at the shore of Lake Berryessa, we pass through huge road-cuts of sedimentary rock whose bedding planes, originally horizontal, have been bent almost ninety degrees and are nearly vertical. Reaching for the sky in distinct unrumpled stripes, the rock ends in hog-backs, jagged ridges. Cretaceous in age, these are the bottom layers of the Great Valley Sequence, bent high enough to resemble the bleaching ribs of a shipwreck. They are some of the strata that were folded against the Franciscan mélange when it rose (or was pushed) to the surface as the latest addition to the western end of the continent. In the heat and pressure of the Farallon Trench, the Franciscan sediments had been metamorphosed to varying extents, with the result that when they ultimately appeared on the surface they were miscellaneous and heterogeneous well beyond the brink of chaos. This lithic compote is the essence of the Coast Ranges. You leave the precise bedding planes and jagged ridgelines of the Great Valley Sequence and enter a country of precipitous notes and rootless outcrops resting in scaly clay. In its lumpiness it resembles a glacial topography magnified many times. If the Great Valley Sequence can be compared to regimental stripes, the Franciscan is paisley.

"Look at this munged-up Franciscan glop!" Moores exclaims.

Narrow thoroughfares twist among the giddy hills. Ink Grade Road. Dollarhide Road.

"Look at that mélange! Holy moly, look at the lumps!"

Between the grinding lithospheric plates, the rock of this terrain was so pervasively sheared that a roadcut in metabasalt looks like green hamburger. We clearly see its contact with the scaly clay.

"That clay is the matrix of the Franciscan, in which blobs of various material are everywhere contained, and that is the guts of the Coast Range story. The metabasalt is a tectonic block in the matrix. You can see why people who tried to map stratigraphy went crazy. Imagine—before plate tectonics—the aching problems that this fruitcake, this raisins-in-a-pudding kind of stuff, produced. It doesn't fit the stratigraphic rules we all grew up on. It was assumed that you had a stratigraphic sequence here, and for years people tried un-successfully to explain these places in terms of eroded and deformed stratigraphies. In 1965, Ken Hsü proposed the mélange idea. But he suggested that the mélange had come here by gravity—that it had slid off the Sierra. No one had the idea of underthrusting—what we now see as the subduction of one plate beneath another, with all this miscellaneous material being scraped together and otherwise accumulating at the edge of the overriding plate. In 1969, Warren Hamilton of the U.S.G.S. published a paper on the underflow of the Pacific crust beneath North America in Cretaceous and Cenozoic time. He presented the paper at the Penrose conference on the new global tectonics. Suddenly, people had a new view of the Franciscan. They said, 'Oh, that must be a berm resulting from subduction.' And the whole story broke open."

The Franciscan mélange contains rock of such widespread provenance that it is quite literally a collection from the entire Pacific basin, or even half of the surface of the planet. As fossils and paleomagnetism indicate, there are sediments from continents (sandstones and so forth) and rocks from scattered marine sources (cherts, graywackes, serpentines, gabbros, pillow lavas, and other volcanics) assembled at random in the matrix clay. Caught between the plates in the subduction, many of these things were taken down 65,000 to 100,000 feet and spit back up as blue schist. This dense, heavy blue-gray rock, characteristic of subduction zones wherever found, is raspberried with garnets.

In a 1973 paper by Kenneth Jingwha Hsü appears a sentence describing the Franciscan mélange—this 500-mile formation, the structural nature of which he was the first to recognize—in terms that could be applied to almost any extended family sitting down to a Thanksgiving dinner:

> These Mesozoic rocks are characterized by a general destruction of original junctions, whether igneous structures or sedimentary bedding, and by the shearing down of the more ductile material until it functions as a matrix in which fragments of the more brittle rocks float as isolated lenticlesor boudins.

Hsü was born in China and began to use his umlaut as a tenured professor at the Swiss Federal Institute of Technology.

The mélange above Auburn, which collected against North America before the arrival of the Smartville Block, tells the same sort of story as the Franciscan, with the difference that the rock in the Sierra mélange has been almost wholly recrystallized, as a result of the collisions that completed California. Kodiak Island and the Shumagin Islands are accretionary wedges, too—shoved against Alaska by the northbound Pacific Plate. The Oregon coast is an accretionary wedge (the Juan de Fuca Plate versus the North American Plate), complicated by a chain of seamounts that have come drifting in, making, among other things, Oregon's spectacular sea stacks. The outer islands of Indonesia are accretionary berms like the California Coast Ranges (the Australian Plate versus the Eurasian Plate), not to mention the

Apennines of Italy, the north coast of the Gulf of Oman, and the Arakan ranges of Burma.

Now and again in the Coast Ranges you see ophiolite pillows on top of the mélange—a typical relationship, since the mélange forms at the edge of the overriding plate and the ophiolite is already on the overriding plate, having been previously emplaced there. Ocean-crustal detritus is widespread and prominent among the rocks of the Franciscan, but the Coast Range Ophiolite, in more concentrated form, is in the eastern part of the mountains, where it has been bent upward with the overlying Great Valley sediments, and pretty much shattered. Between Davis and Rutherford is a block of serpentine—disjunct, floating in the Franciscan—that underlies the bowl of a small mountain valley. The serpentine has weathered into soil, now planted to vines. These are some of the few grapes in California that are grown in the soil of the state rock. Moores is predisposed toward the wine. To him, its bouquet is ophiolitic, its aftertaste slow to part with serpentine's lingering mystery. To me, it tastes less of the deep ocean than of low tide. The stuff is fermented peridotite—a Mohorivicic red with the lustre of chromium.

The winery is in the deep shade of redwoods on a tertiary road. It makes only 10,000 gallons and has been in one family for a hundred years. The cave is in Franciscan sandstone. The kegs, tanks, and barrels are wood. Outside the cave, we stand on a wooden deck looking into a steep valley through the trunks of the big trees. Passing a glass under his nose, Moores remarks that the aroma is profound and reminds him of the wines of Cyprus. There is an intact ophiolite on the side of Mount St. Helena, at the northwest end of the Napa Valley, he tells me—an almost complete sequence, capped with sediments but lacking pillows. There's a complete sequence on the east side of Mount Diablo. "If you mapped the Coast Range Ophiolite, it would go from Oregon all the way down, in discontinuous blobs, plus the shards you see around San Francisco and elsewhere—rocks of the ophiolitic suite that just lie around as broken pieces, like the block that is under these grapes, and cannot be read in sequence." When Moores was first in California, he happened upon a report about mercury deposits at the north end of the Napa Valley. It mentioned "gabbro...along the contact between serpentine and volcanics." Moores got into his van, went to the Napa Valley, and looked. He then interested Steven Bezore, a graduate student, in working there. Bezore's master's thesis was the first demonstration of an ophiolitic complex in California, and led to the recognition of the Coast Range Ophiolite. After the winery, we stop at a crossroads store, Moores explaining that he requires coffee "to back-titrate the wine."

The descent is deep to the floor of the Napa Valley, which is flat. For a Coast Range valley, it is also spacious—as much as three miles wide. Vines cover it. Up the axis runs the two-lane St. Helena Highway, which seems to be lined with movie sets. This road is the vague but startling equivalent of the Route des Vins from Gevrey-Chambertin to Meursault through Beaune. The apparent stage sets are agricultural Disneylands: Beringer's Gothic half-timber Rhine House, Christian Brothers' Laotian Buddhist monastic château, Robert Mondavi's Spanish mission. Most offer tours, and wines to sip. As a day progresses, tongues thicken on the St. Helena Highway, where the traffic begins to weave in the late morning and is a war zone by midafternoon. The safest sippers are in stretch limos, which seem to outnumber Chevrolets.

Most valleys in the Coast Ranges are smaller and higher than this one, their typical altitude at least a thousand feet. The southern end of the Napa Valley, being close to the San Francisco bays, is essentially at sea level. The valley floor rises with distance from the water, but not much. St. Helena, in the north-central part of the Napa Valley, has an elevation of 255 feet. It is surrounded by mountains that are comparable in height to the Green Mountains of Vermont or the White Mountains of New Hampshire. Why this deep hole in such a setting?

The San Andreas family of faults is spread through the Coast Ranges, and outlying members are beneath the Great Valley. Where a transform fault develops a releasing bend—which is not uncommon—the bend will pull apart as the two sides move, opening a sort of parallelogram, which, among soft mountains, will soon be vastly deeper than an ordinary water-sculpted valley. In the Coast Ranges, most depressions are high and erosional. Some are deep tectonic valleys that are known in geology as pull-apart basins. In the Napa region, Sonoma Valley, Ukiah Valley, Willits Valley, and Round Valley are also pull-apart basins. Lake Berryessa lies in a pull-apart basin, and so does Clear Lake.

Where pull-apart basins develop—stretching and thinning the local crust, drawing the mantle closer to the surface—volcanic eruptions cannot be far behind. In the Pliocene, after the Farallon Trench at this latitude ceased to operate and the San Andreas family appeared, the Napa basin had scarcely pulled itself apart before the fresh red rhyolite lavas and air-fall tuffs poured in. The Coast Ranges were aglow with sulphurous volcanism, its products hardening upon the Franciscan. The nutritive soils derived from these rocks prepared the geography of wine.

The rocks are known in geology as the Sonoma Volcanics. Napa and Sonoma are Patwin Indian names: "Napa" means house; "Sonoma" means nose or the Land of Chief Nose. The rocks are the Land of Chief Nose Volcanics. Chief Nose was a Tastevin before his time. The heat of the volcanics lingers in the mud baths and hot springs of Calistoga. The heat lingers under cleared woods near Mount St. Helena, where small power stations dot the high ground like isolated geothermal farms.

As the new fault system wrenched the country, fissures opened, and hot groundwater burst out in the form of geysers and springs. They precipitated cryptocrystalline quartz and—in this matrix—various metals. Some gold. More silver. Near the surface, easiest to mine, were brilliant red crystals of cinnabar (mercuric sulphide). Mercury will effectively pluck up gold from crushed ores. In the nineteenth century, the Coast Ranges were tunnelled for mercury. It was carried across the Great Central Valley and used in the Sierra. The gold of the Coast Ranges was in those days insignificant but is more than significant now. In the 1980s, the Homestake Mining Company dug two open pits in ridges north of the Napa Valley. In surface area, they aggregate roughly a square mile. The gold is too fine to be seen through a microscope but is nonetheless there in sufficient con-centration to be dissolved economically with cyanide. Homestake's underground mine in the Black Hills of South Dakota is about a century old, and at latest count was 6,800 feet deep—the deepest mine in the Western Hemisphere. Homestake has produced more gold than any corporation in North America. With these new claims in the Coast Ranges, the company has more than doubled its reserves.

In 1880, Robert Louis Stevenson—aged thirty, newly married, consumptive—fled the "poisonous fog" of San Francisco and went into the mountains above Calistoga, where he and his American bride and her twelve-year-old son spent the summer squatting in an empty cabin at a closed-down mine called Silverado. From their high bench among rusting machinery and rubbled tailings, they looked down into the green rectangles of the Napa Valley.

> The floor of the valley is extremely level to the roots of the hills; only here and there a hillock, crowned with pines, rises like the barrow of some chieftain famed in war.

Stevenson had more than a passing sense of the geology.

> Here, indeed, all is new, nature as well as towns. The very hills of California have an unfinished look; the rains and streams have not yet carved them to their perfect shape.

Hot Springs and White Sulphur Springs are the names of two stations on the Napa Valley railroad; and Calistoga itself seems to repose on a mere film above a boiling, subterranean lake.

He began making notes for what became *The Silverado Squatters* and various settings for later work. He described the summit Mount St. Helena as "a cairn of quartz and cinnabar." He noted that Calistoga was a coined name. A Mormon promoter had been thinking of America's premier spa. Fortunately, his idea failed to travel, or there would be a Nevastoga, a Utastoga, a Wyostoga. Rattlesnakes resounded in the air like crickets. For a couple of months, Stevenson didn't know what he was hearing.

The rattle has a legendary credit; it is said to be awe-inspiring, and, once heard, to stamp itself forever in the memory. But the sound is not at all alarming; the hum of many insects, and the buzz of the wasp convince the ear of danger quite as readily. As a matter of fact, we lived for weeks in Silverado, coming and going, with rattles sprung on every side and it never occurred to us to be afraid. I used to take sun-baths and do calisthenics in a certain pleasant nook among azalea and calcanthus, the rattles whizzing on every side like spinning-wheels, and the combined hiss or buzz rising louder and angrier at any sudden movement but I was never in the least impressed, nor ever attacked. It was only towards the end of our stay that a man down at Calistoga, who was expatiating on the terrifying nature of the sound, gave me at last a very good imitation, and it burst on me at once that we dwelt in the very metropolis of deadly snakes, and that the rattle was simply the commonest noise in Silverado.

Without so much as a warning rattle, the owner of the Silverado Mine turned up one day, discovering and embarrassing the illegal squatter.

I somewhat quailed. I hastened to do him fealty, said I
gathered he was the Squattee....

Stevenson's summer was four years after the Battle of the Little
Bighorn. The West was that old. Yet he counted fifty vineyards in the
Napa Valley. Farmers had been in the valley for nearly half a century.
In the 1830s, George Yount, of North Carolina, had been converted
to Catholicism and had had himself baptized Jorge Concepcion
Yount in order to obtain a Mexican land grant of almost 12,000 acres.
An English surgeon to whom the Mexicans also gave a Napa Valley
land grant named his place Rancho Carne Humana. In 1876, the
Beringer winery was founded by Germans from Mainz. In approximate
replication of their ancestral home, they built Rhine House in 1883.
The stretch limos park there now, beside wide lawns under tall elms.
Off the jump seats come people who go inside and lay down forty
dollars for the magnum opus "Beringer: A Napa Valley Legend."
Leafing through the book, Moores picks up the information that the
foundation and first story of Rhine House are limestone. He goes
outside and squints at the house through his ten-power Hastings
Triplet. "Jesus Christ!" he says. For Moores, this is new ground. He
has never before seen limestone that came out of a volcano. "It's
poorly welded volcanic ash with lots of big vesicles, pumice lapilli,"
he goes on. "It's friable volcanic ash! A welded tuff! An ignimbrite!"

Louis Martini's cement-block roadhouse, south of St. Helena
on the way to Rutherford, is a low, clean-lined, postroad-modern
building that lacks windows and has a long portico and a few
wrought-iron lamps. Its architectural statement is upper-middle
prime rib. Among the building's tiled rooms are showcases of Martini
wines and a long, dark bar. No one hurries anyone away, and in the
cool quiet we sample half a dozen bottles, talking geology with our
noses in the outcrop. Louis Martini's wines are straightforward,
stalwart, allusive, volcanic. They are prepared to travel—like the
terrane they derive from, and like the first Martini (who emigrated

from Italy in 1894), and, according to Moores, like Italy itself, which departed from Europe in the Jurassic but later went home. Italy became a prong of Africa, he says, cupping his hand and orbiting a Cabernet Sauvignon. Italy left Europe, joined Africa, and later smashed back into Europe in the collision that made the Alps. The quarried Tuscan serpentines in the walls of the Duomo and the Giotto campanile are particles of the ophiolites that underscore this story.

Martini's Pinot Noir has the brawny overtones of an upland Rioja, the resilient spring of an athletic Médoc. Moores wonders if I have noticed that "the Claret coast of France" and the Cantabrian coast of northern Spain seem to suggest an open bivalve, with Bordeaux at the hinge. In the early Cretaceous, when the Atlantic was young and narrow, there was no water between western France and northern Spain; the hinge was closed. The whole of Iberia got caught up in the spreading, and was perhaps yanked by Africa as Africa moved northeast. A rift opened and widened, and became the Bay of Biscay. In a comparatively short time, the Iberian Peninsula swung ninety degrees and assumed its present position.

During the Zinfandel, Moores summarizes the United Kingdom as "the remnants of a collision that occurred at the end of the Silurian." Mélanges resembling the Franciscan were caught in it, he says—for example, Caernarvonshire and Anglesey, in Wales. Collisional ranges appeared, later to be dismembered by the opening of the ocean. In France, the Massif Central is actually a continuation of the northern Appalachians. The southern Appalachians go up to New Jersey and then jump to North Africa as the Atlas Mountains and then to the Iberian plateau and to the Pyrenees, which were later enhanced by compressions that developed as Spain swung around.

During the Napa Valley Reserve Petite Sirah, I mention the Brooks Range, where I have recently been.

The Brooks Range, Moores says, is a sliver of exotic continental material that came in from above Alaska, hit a subduction zone, and put ophiolite sequences along what is now the south slope. In the collision that followed, the exotic sliver was folded into mountains.

"When was that?"

"I forget. In the Jurassic, probably, or the early Cretaceous.

The Seward Peninsula—where Nome is, in west-central Alaska—is a piece of Jurassic blue schist surrounded by ophiolitic rock, but no one knows where the Seward Peninsula came from. For that matter, he adds, there is no certainty about where any of Alaska came from. It seems to consist entirely of exotic pieces that drifted to North America in Mesozoic time. South of the Denali Fault, which runs east-west and is close to Mount McKinley, is the huge terrane that geologists call Wrangellia. It was an island arc, developed over an ocean plateau. Moores describes Mount McKinley as "a bit of granite" that came up into Wrangellia after it arrived. Not long ago, Japan was attached to Asia. It drifted away. Japan is coming toward North America one centimetre a year. It may be a part of Alaska in eight hundred million years.

There is a shift change at Louis Martini's. One hostess replaces another. The new one says to her departing colleague, "Be careful out there. It's intense. They're driving all over the road."

To Vincent Van Gogh of the House He Painted in 1890, the Year of His Death

Jane Mead

This evening my valley has the colors
of your "House at Auvers"—your colors,
my colors now. Fog smudges up from the bay
and is lost in the blue-green fields—
it's the color of the lake through mist, color
of the smoke from five damp trash fires
which drifts up towards elsewhere, taking
its time. This is the color you gave
your sky, this is the color you gave
your house. The greens I see are the ones *you* chose
for roof and shrubs and shutters, and I—

in my red flannel shirt—could be
the flame of poppies you put in the corner.

Except that nothing human strays there—
there is no sign of human life at all.

I have come from planting blackberries,
sunflowers and cabbages—planting them
to hold me here a while longer,
in this house overlooking the valley.

The valley is fading in dusk and warm rain.

All the houses are dropping away. They are leaving
too fast. What if we never have our moment?

And what if it's all there—in your painting—
what if there *is* no missing gesture? What
if a shovel left by the gate would not have done,
if putting it there could not have saved you?

And if it's *not* the absence in your windows
of a frail hand pulling curtains back,
of a face, half-shadowed, looking toward you—
then it must be that you knew too well
just how to make the sagging woodshed lovely.

The world is still much larger than itself.
The world is still unbearable or small:
greens, blues, flame of poppies, smoke
rising up toward elsewhere—taking its time.

Where the Zinfandel Pass Their Seasons in Mute Rows

The night Ed died, my father
wrenched his own
cracked, yellow molars
from his mouth and went
crashing like a wounded deer
over the ridge and down,
five miles through the brush,
into Soda Canyon where the cops
found him wandering, spent,
around the burnt-out dance hall
and brought him home.

Bandaging his brush cuts,
I noticed how he is becoming
the sharp-bodied boy he was
when he ran these hills
until he knew them better
than he knew his own father,
who knew them better than
the shape of *his* father's hands.

Then I watched him bend into sleep—
embryo of the king bed,
fetus with dust guts.

On the day of Ed's funeral
he gave me those teeth
"for earrings" he said, "no good
to Ed, or even to me, now."

We buried Ed with manzanita
and bay, those plants
he loved most—our own wish
for *something* to hold forever,
some way to be, in the end,
anything but alone and incomplete.

This dawn I walked
the red mud, looking
for something I could know
would never leave me—
out through the vineyard
where my father tempts life
from dirt to wine in a habit
of seasons stronger than love.
Setting my palms into the mud
at the base of a gnarled vine,
I pressed them together
and whispered "speak."
But the vine's silence just grew
into the silence of the dead
who once tended it.

Then I saw exactly how
it was beautiful—
how it held its world whole
beneath its fog-slick bark,

while the things we ask
to hold us leave us
spent. My handprints in the mud
filled with water and melted
away and my palms—done with prayer,
held out between the earth
and the sky—were empty
and red, and drying into a map.
I flexed them. The rivers widened.

Wine Country

David Bromige

We live in wine country.
We have developed corkscrew skills.
We wipe the inside necks of bottles.
Improvise a vocabulary

Upon the obdurate clichés
We've squinted at on labels.
Together we've heard vinous bells
Ring out for couples who are happy—

And sometimes the merry
Have been us, in the white-gold hills

Buck naked, Pan and Bacchante to the gills—
Ring out also for those we came to bury,

Bereaved hearts easing grief with wine. Many
Merry, many mournful, mouthfuls,
Glasses drained until our skulls
Whirled with the world, so lightly

We knew ourselves one with Eternity,
Looked in each other's eyes, lulled
With our love again revealed.
Dawns came, bringing, doubly heavy,

Our heads into the real, the really
Rotten world. Or half of world.
As we have been often told,
You can't, on only one wing, fly:

And so here we sit, you and I,
With a redwood table steadied
Between us, our glasses readied:
We who live in wine country,

Half-filled, half-emptied.
Praise to the volatile
Nectar mouthful by mouthful,
We laughed and laughed and cried,

In wine-country where we died
Where we had lived, and always will.

from Carson Valley

Bill Barich

On Sunday, Arthur Atwater was at peace, thankful for some time off from work. He had no precise memory of his last such break. It seemed as historical to him as the Peloponnesian War he had once studied in school. Over a rare unhurried breakfast, he caught up on his mail and browsed through the accumulated catalogs, deciding he would reward himself with a new down vest when the crush was over. He clipped his neglected toe- and fingernails, showered, and put on some clean underwear, then dusted the dogs with flea powder before brewing a second pot of tea. His log was before him on the table, and when he thumbed through his entries for the year, he was impressed by the sheer bulk of them. Here was a literal record of his efforts, testimony to the fact that he had done his job, or at least had tried to.

> Sunday, Oct. 6th. White grapes all in now, with top dollar due on the Chardonnay. Cloudy and cool this a.m., a light breeze from the north. We start picking Cabs tomorrow, tested out at 23.1 yesterday. Zins almost ready, will come up fast if it gets warm, could be trouble. Some pretty color in the leaves. Fall, I guess. I missed it.

He had no plans for his day off except to relax, but his thoughts kept revolving around the harvest and all those red grapes about to pop. After a while, he copied some figures onto a legal tablet and drove into town to deliver another of his progress reports to Victor Torelli, but the old man refused to even acknowledge him this trip, being hypnotically devoted to a '49ers football game. His recliner was pushed up close to a fireplace that was throwing out enough BTUs to melt paint. Atwater left him to a mean household temperature of about eighty-five degrees and stopped at Charlie Grimes's farm on his way home to borrow a back-up fanbelt for his tractor. He found Charlie and a local winemaker sampling some grape juice, green and frothy and fresh from a press. The winemaker passed the beaker under his nose.

"Go on and taste it," Grimes commanded him. "It won't kill you, Arthur."

Atwater took a sip and swirled it in his mouth. "Chardonnay," he said, smacking his lips. "Very nice. The flavor's real strong. Apples, definitely. Maybe a touch of citrus."

"Those grapes were goddam perfect. If you want a thirty-dollar bottle of wine, come back here in three years."

"I'll mark it down on my calendar."

"You had better. Because we'll be sold out in an eyeblink." Grimes pressed a knuckle to a nostril and blew some snot toward a pumice of grape skins on the floor. "You pull off any blacks yet?" he asked, subjecting his other nostril to the same unblocking.

"Not yet. Tomorrow we start. I'm itchy about it, to tell you the truth."

"How they looking?"

"The Cabs are just right. The Zins need some more heat."

"I don't envy you, no sir," Grimes said, clucking his tongue. "I had a year like that in nineteen and eighty-three. Every goddam black grape was ready all at once. They was pelting me like hailstones."

"They come at you hard and fast, don't they?"

"The co-op I belonged to then, those people were backed up for hours. One fellow, he had a hammock strung under his flatbed so he could take naps. I about expired myself."

"But you lived to tell the tale."

"Some would have it."

They proceeded to a toolshed where Grimes stored a truly monumental selection of spare parts. Atwater watched him rudely tossing aside spark plugs and oil filters to unearth a litter of fanbelts. They moved off into the light and walked past the barn. It was inordinately white and loomed over the property like a hole in the sky that needed to be filled.

"You going to leave your barn that way?" Atwater asked.

"No, I'll do something with it sooner or later," Grimes told him. "But I'm not about to rush myself. Creative ideas, they don't come easy."

"You're a true artist, Charlie."

Grimes showed unusual humility. "It's been said before."

Atwater motored around his own vineyard that afternoon and tasted some Zinfandel grapes from different rows. One from the inside of a cluster and one from the outside, one from the cane and one from the head. He chewed, spat, and ticked off the seconds to gauge how long the flavor held, how richly it was concentrated—four, seven, even ten seconds. It would be a fine vintage, he thought, and would produce big red wines of a decisive varietal character. He lay down to rest on a hilltop after that, sampling what it felt like to be lazy, his hands cupped behind his head and his imagination streaking toward Anna in faraway New York as it often did at such undefended moments. He saw her striding down a broad boulevard and cutting a swath through the crowd, like a bright flame. He loved how she burned. He smiled to himself and understood to his astonishment that he must have forgiven her. It was possible he'd forgiven himself, too. There was a new clarity in the air, and he allowed himself to think he'd been right not to extinguish that tiny flicker of hope.

"Oh bullshit, Atwater," he shouted to an audience of grapes and crows, disgusted with himself. "Bullshit, bullshit, bullshit!" Besides, he'd been busy in bed with that bartender from The Rib Room.

Early the next morning, in the gnawing dark, he dressed and listened for the familiar sounds of his crew arriving, the coughing and the joking, but the vineyard was unnaturally quiet. He listened more intently and heard a muted drone and then nothing more. The pickers must be waiting to be told when and where to begin on the red grapes, he figured, so he shot through the door without a bite to eat and hustled toward some human shapes who were still in the process of emerging from the fading night. They were glancing nervously about, as if to locate in the shadows a presence to give them an assurance they seemed to require.

Atwater saw the reason why. Antonio Lopez was missing. "*Donde está Antonio?*" he asked them.

His question was met with shrugs and downcast eyes.

"*Dígame la verdad,*" he repeated. "*Donde está Antonio?*"

"Not here, *señor!*" somebody piped up.

"*Desaparecido,*" another voice added. Lopez had disappeared, and nobody knew his whereabouts.

There was no time for further discussion. Every lost second would be tallied on the negative side of the ledger, Atwater knew. He led the crew to the ripest block of Cabernet Sauvignon, distributed the hosed-down plastic tubs, and got everybody started. He noticed then that Omar Perez was also missing, as were all three Hernandezes. He was short a total of five pickers, and that meant he would harvest far fewer lugs on the day. An average of about thirty lugs per picker, so one hundred and fifty times thirty-five pounds a lug—the rough calculation came to about five thousand pounds of grapes. All those grapes would remain on the vine, fruit that was very nearly at its peak and under a threat of raisining if Atwater didn't correct the shortfall in manpower as quickly as he could.

The pickers sensed that something had gone haywire. Deprived of their routine, they were acting contrary. They dawdled, cut corners, and competed among themselves instead of helping one another. Without Lopez to supervise them and set a pace, they were in rebellion.

"What's going on here?" Atwater asked Rudolfo Mendez, who seemed not to be moving at all. "*Que pasa?*"

Mendez pointed solemnly. He had a row that curved uphill and didn't want to do any climbing.

"Well, shit, go pick over there, then," Atwater told him, shoving him toward level ground.

But Mendez wouldn't budge. He nodded malignly at the picker in the row next to him. "*Me esta sigiuendo,*" he griped.

"I won't let him follow you. Just go!"

Atwater broke for his trailer and phoned Lopez at home. He got no answer, only a dull, distant, uninterrupted ringing. He returned to the vineyard in a fury and caught Serena Cedillo hastily dumping her full tub into a harvest bin and dashing off before he could speak to her. Hoisting himself above the rim of the bin, he saw why. It was filled with grapes that were mashed, split, and leaking juice. The juice would oxidize and cause some fermentation, so he leaned over and plucked away the damaged clusters. He tossed out the imperfect ones, too, those with shot, puckered, or shriveled berries that should have been left on the vine. The pickers were grabbing anything at all without regard to quality.

Atwater whistled loudly to call a halt. The crew gathered to face him, dragging their heels. They were cantankerous and wouldn't look at him when he held up a flawed cluster and ordered them not to pick such grapes. It was useless, he thought. They were beyond caring and would continue to do as they pleased.

"*Ándale!*" he yelled with fake enthusiasm, clapping his hands. "*Ándale! Ándale!*"

He left the farm to search for some replacements. He scoured Carson Valley Road, but the men who'd been loitering in strategic positions just yesterday had hired on somewhere or had merely given up and gone home to Mexico. Ordinarily, idlers were as thick as flies in front of Roy's Market, but Atwater didn't see a single person there. He tried all the cabins as well, banging on every door, and failed to rouse anybody, except for a surly fellow who sat by himself near a window in cabin four, playing solitaire and sipping from a bottle of Johnny Walker.

"I've got work," Atwater told him, as if that were the best news the fellow could ever hear. "I need a picker."

"I am no interest in picking."

"I'll go to a dollar and a half a lug for the right man."

"*Qué lástima!* I am the captain, *señor.*"

Atwater made for the farm again, having exhausted his prospects for the moment. He consoled himself with thoughts of all the things that might have gone wrong for Antonio Lopez, the many minor impediments that could have forced him to be late, an emergency involving his car or his daughter or even his stomach that would surely be fixed by now. So vehemently did he pursue this fantasy that he expected Lopez's old Toyota to be parked in its usual spot, but he was mistaken. The rebellion in his vineyard had become more entrenched, in fact. Two men had put down their tubs and stopped picking altogether, crouching in the shade as if to set a desultory example for the other crew members to follow. They had not so much quit their jobs as gone out on strike, Atwater surmised, since they were still on the property and so were still open to negotiation.

"Yes?" He addressed them as graciously as he could under the circumstances. "*Hay algun problema?*"

"*Me he torcido la muñeca,*" the first picker replied. His wrist was sprained.

"*Me duele todo el cuerpo,*" said the second picker. His entire body hurt.

They had more grievances, too. Atwater knelt next to them and heard them out, his expression one of utmost concern. These new red grapes were much smaller than the old white grapes and were concealed more intricately and deviously in trickier foliage, the pickers claimed. Even if a man pushed himself to the limit, he still could not earn as much money as he had earned on the old white grapes. That was nature's fault, of course, and not the boss's, both pickers agreed, but it was still unjust and unacceptable. At other vineyards, the boss used a blower to remove the leaves in advance and make the picking easier. The whole crew was discouraged, in pain, sick at heart.

"*Yo comprendo,*" Atwater told them, drawing circles in the dirt with a twig. He explained that he felt pity for the pickers—how could he not, being a laborer himself?—but the *patrón* had to make a profit for the farm to survive. He couldn't afford any special equipment to blow away the leaves. The *patrón* was a person of high honor and integrity, though, and he wouldn't want his crew to suffer unduly, so five dollars would be added to everyone's pay at the end of the day.

"Five dollars?"

"Every day?"

Atwater confirmed it. The grinning pickers congratulated one another by shaking hands. They were cured miraculously and simultaneously of their ailments and trotted into the vineyard to spread the word.

The raise in pay greased the wheels of commerce. The harvest machine and all its component parts clicked back into gear and began to run at optimum speed once more, with each important movement falling as if by divine intervention into its appropriate groove. There was a smoothness to the flow again, and Atwater permitted himself a moment of pride, congratulating himself for being a genius bilingual mediator who had saved his crop from certain failure. In the mesh of shadow and light, he could hear a distinct hum that was the hallmark of a harvest going well.

He hauled his first load of red grapes, eight-plus tons, to the winery late that afternoon and had to wait for more than an hour in a line of trucks that extended beyond the horizon, but he was grateful enough just to be there. The fields were dark on his return. He spent his evening on the phone talking to neighboring growers and asking for some help. Again and again he tried to reach Antonio Lopez, without any success. The silence nagged at him, but he was too tired to go hunting for his foreman in the wilds of Santa Rosa. Something very bad must have happened, he had to admit.

Morning brought with it a promise of deliverance. Atwater woke with a surge of unanticipated energy, his spirits refreshed by a good night's sleep. The weather was warmer, and the world looked gentler around the edges, rosier and more accommodating, robbed of its menace. He wished that he had a football to throw in homage to the glories of autumn. With his right arm, he performed a quarterback's feint and pretended to release an arching spiral toward the sky. He saw that a few pickers were already at work, while others drank coffee and prepared themselves. He counted heads and was delighted to find that he had not lost anyone. Some new men were present, too. On loan from Charlie Grimes was a stocky old veteran he knew simply as Manuel, and Dick Rhodes had sent him a pair of young brothers just in from Oregon, where they had harvested apples and pears in the orchards around Medford.

The brothers had never picked any grapes before, so Atwater conducted a tutorial. They were fast learners, skillful with their knives and eager to satisfy. Manuel, on the other hand, needed no instruction at all. He was an imperturbable master of his craft and could be trusted to keep the crew on its best behavior. Atwater assigned him the task of maintaining order and walked over to run a test on a block of hillside Zinfandel. His refractometer showed him in empirical terms what he had suspected. The warming trend was affecting the sugar level in the grapes. It was rising rapidly. Soon he would be swimming in ripe fruit, tons of it, so he decided to rig a trailer behind the flatbed truck for double hauling, outfitting it with four gondolas instead of two. That way he'd make just one trip to the winery daily instead of two or three and wouldn't waste his precious time waiting in line.

The pickers worked straight through the noon hour, fueling themselves with snacks eaten on the fly. The fruit was coming off nicely now, still smoothly, and they refused to break the rhythm for fear that they could never capture it again. Their efforts were all of a piece, braided together toward a common goal. They were inside the harvest machine and looked unstoppable, Atwater thought. Sweat poured from them and streaked their faces, and grime and dust coated their arms. The men had stripped down to t-shirts that were stained and spotted with purple blotches, while the women wore broad-brimmed straw hats and had knotted kerchiefs and bandannas around their necks to protect themselves from the brutal sun.

Atwater stayed apart. He was busy on his tractor and emptied one bin after another into his gondolas. The rig was capacious and would hold upward of twenty tons of grapes. Around three o'clock, with every muscle in his body stretched to its elastic limits, he took a breather, drove to Roy's, and brought back some cases of cold beer and soda to invigorate the crew. He packed the cans in two buckets, layered them with cracked ice, and toted them from row to row, saying, "Here you go, here's something to kill that taste of dust, here you go, have yourself a cold drink."

"We are a winning team!" Manuel hoisted a can and toasted the other pickers with an impromptu cheer. "Teamwork!"

"*Eso es!*"

Atwater pressed a frigid Coke to his forehead like a compress and smiled. "You're a goddam wonderful team, if you ask me," he told them all. "You saved my bacon."

"Wonderful team."

"We save the bacon!" There was merriment all around.

Back to work the pickers went, pushing themselves, enduring. The sun dropped toward the far hills, and the valley floor was rich with a last incandescent torrent of light so powerful that it added a patina of burnished color to everybody's skin. Every tinge of red in the soil, every lateritic particle, grew bright. Atwater watched his crew slow to a crawl. They were in a trance and stared out as though at a fiery hearth. When Serena Cedillo took off her straw hat, shook out her hair, and combed the tangles from it with rough strokes, the light caught in each auburn strand and rippled about her in an aura. The sun kept dropping until it became an orange disc balanced atop some pines and firs on a distant ridge, and then it was abruptly gone, guttered out, and shadows fell across the vineyard. The thump of buckets went on, but the lively racket of voices began to die down.

The brothers from Oregon were the first to call it quits. Stoical to the core, they showed off the raw and bloody blisters on their hands, but they vowed to return in the morning anyway and were praised for their manly attitude, their simple courage. Others followed them shortly, shouting farewells, stowing away their grape knives, and collecting the sweaters and jackets that they had cast aside or hung on grape stakes in the heat of the day. As they walked doggedly from the vineyard, they had the thoroughly depleted look of athletes at the close of a grueling contest, Atwater thought, winners who had barely snatched a victory from the jaws of defeat.

It was a little past six o'clock when he started for the CV outlet to deliver his monster load of grapes. The drive would take him about twenty minutes. He flipped on his headlights in the gathering dusk. The gondolas rumbled noisily behind his truck and swayed with the weight of his cargo, filled up nearly to the brim. He didn't know for sure how many tons of fruit he was hauling—seventeen, eighteen, it could have been a full twenty tons. It was a solid payload, at any rate, and it gave him a good feeling in his gut and a sense of money in the bank. He looked out at the dry brown hills and the fields now fading from view and saw everywhere the same comradely scene of dispatch as more and more picking crews unraveled to go their separate ways. The spiraling dust, the arms raised in salute, the figures solitary and committed, all were beautiful to him.

He passed over a creek where a trace of water still trickled and moss slicked about. He was whistling and unaware of it. When he reached the CV outlet, he was shocked to see how many trucks were lined up ahead of him—not only trucks but also many tractors pulling gondolas. It was worse than the previous day by far. The line stretched back across the bridge for hundreds of yards. By craning his neck, Atwater could just make out the lit platform of the sugar shack. He was so far away from the winery proper that he couldn't hear the purr of the crusher or the whine of the transfer pumps that moved the grape juice from tank to tank. All down the line, drivers had climbed from their cabs to wait on the road. In the foul and heavy exhaust fumes from their idling engines, they smoked and talked softly and aimlessly as they passed around a box of doughnuts.

Atwater joined them. "What's the trouble?" he asked.

"Trouble?" he was told. "Trouble is, every red grape in Carson Valley decided to get ripe at the same goddam time."

"Ah, shit, that's just an excuse," another driver said angrily. "They could kick it along a lot faster if they wanted to. I came out with a load this morning and got through in under an hour."

"Everybody's tired," said a third driver. "CV, they weren't prepared for this. They need a whole lot more help. Some of the boys inside, they're about to fall over on their faces."

"Have a doughnut here, pal." Atwater chose a honey glazed from a box and ate it greedily in a couple of bites. "Go on, have another one. There's no reason to starve yourself to death just because you're desperate, is there?"

The line of trucks inched forward. The drivers watched to see if the advance would merit a return to their cabs, but the fleet had only traveled a few feet. So they stayed where they were and chatted and flung about accusations and alibis until the next jump forward opened the space between vehicles a little wider and created an illusion of progress. Atwater climbed up with the rest, shifted into first gear, and drove on for about five yards until he had to stop again. He got down after that and walked past the men on the road as if in a delirium and started counting the trucks ahead of him, but he was soon discouraged. The exercise was pointless. The number of trucks didn't matter. The line, however long it was, would move or not move of its own accord, at a rate of speed over which he had no control. His hopes and desires were immaterial. He resigned himself to waiting.

Whenever a truck that was emptied of its load went by the line on its way out, the liberated driver would honk or give a wave of solidarity, but it happened in time that a truck still piled with grapes passed by the men and disappeared without any fanfare. Atwater stuck his head out the window and listened to the drivers relay news of spoiled and rejected fruit.

"Bunch rot," he heard it said, and "They tried to downgrade him," and "He wouldn't swallow it," and "He told 'em where to shove it."

"What's he going to do now?" Atwater shouted above the rattling trucks.

"Damned if I know. There's nobody else around who's even open. He might as well shovel those grapes into a creekbed."

In about two more hours, Atwater was in clear sight of the sugar shack at last. Six trucks were still in front of him, while three stragglers lagged behind him. He watched a tester on the platform of the shack plunge a corer into a load of grapes to take a reading. The tester was so fatigued and trudged about so sluggishly that he might have been drugged. Atwater felt stiff and ornery himself, severely put upon, and he closed his eyes and slept for a few minutes. When he woke and looked at the shack again, the platform was vacant and the light inside it had gone out. He saw Wade Saunders hustling down a ladder and some workers swinging shut the big wrought-iron gates in front of the winery. He couldn't believe it—he was being locked out. He threw open his door and ran toward Saunders in his heavy work boots, tripping over a sprung lace and shouting, "Wade! Hey, Wade! Hold on!" until Saunders yielded to his cry and spun around on his heels.

Hands on his hips, Atwater leaned forward to catch his breath. "Wade?" he asked. "Where are you going?"

"Home," Saunders told him sharply. "I've been roasting in that shack like a stuck pig since before noon. This heat is the damnedest thing"

"My grapes," Atwater said, still gasping. "Who's going to log me in?"

"You'll have to come back tomorrow, Arthur."

"But I've been waiting almost four hours out here!"

"Well, I'm sorry about that." Saunders cupped a hand around his lighter and fired up a cigarette. "But you can't fault me, can you? Do you know what time it is?"

"I don't have a watch. Past ten?"

"Pretty near. And I'm supposed to shut those gates at nine. You fellows all know that. It's spelled out in your contract, and it's up on that sign right over there."

Atwater felt ambushed. "But I got here way before nine!"

"You saw how busy we were yesterday," Saunders reminded him. "You should have built that into your calculations. To turn up at the last minute, well..."

"The last minute! I just told you, Wade, I've been waiting four hours!" Atwater shrieked. He was almost beside himself, and yet he knew there was some truth to Saunders's accusation. He could have played it safe and brought in smaller loads, but he had chosen to roll the dice and gamble it all on one big double haul. "How dare you say that to me!"

"All right, I stand corrected. But you only see your side of things, Arthur. This situation, it happens once in a lifetime. It took CV by complete surprise!"

Atwater pointed to his cargo. "Those are the best grapes in Carson Valley. I remember how bad you wanted them."

"I won't deny it, but I have to draw the line somewhere, don't I?" Saunders asked. "Else there won't ever be an end to it. Look!"

Another truck had pulled up to the winery, piloted by a driver even more ill-fated and behind schedule than the others who were still waiting

"Cut me some slack, Wade," Atwater begged. "Do me just this one favor, and I'll never ask you for another."

"I couldn't cut you any slack even if I wanted to," Saunders replied, his voice raspy. "I've done all the favors I can get away with for one day. You see those workers by the gates? They're on time and a half. It's costing me money just to talk to you."

"Only ten of us are left. At most, it'd take you another half hour."

"I wish I could help you, Arthur, but I can't. The winery's closed, and that's all she wrote."

Atwater grabbed Saunders by the arm. "My grapes will turn overnight in this heat, Wade."

Saunders yanked his arm back. "And you want to hang the blame on me." He chuckled and shook his head at the irony. "Isn't that the shits?"

"I'm not blaming anybody."

"The hell you aren't. Every goddam one of you fellows makes me out to be the scapegoat. Since when am I responsible for your errors in judgment, Arthur? Since when is that? The fact is, you weren't paying attention. Hundreds of trucks have run through here today without a problem. It's your goddam fault, brother, not mine."

"The winery's never been this crowded."

"I guess I get blamed for that, too. Okay. I accept it. Go right ahead and hang it on me."

"Come on, Wade." Atwater hated himself for groveling. "Just this once. Just ten more trucks."

"There'll be eleven by the time I open again."

Atwater swallowed hard. "Have it your way, then," he said, seeing that it was a lost cause. "But do you have to be such a prick about it?"

"Excuse me?"

"You enjoy turning us away. You're being a prick about it."

"Is that what I am?" Saunders looked outraged. "A prick? When I already stayed open an hour past closing time to help out a couple dozen growers? I can't save everybody in the world! The only people who think Wade Saunders is a prick are the ten assholes left in line."

The other drivers got wind of the conversation. They climbed down and came at Saunders with pleas of their own.

"Well, it may look simple to you," Saunders told them slowly, as if they were dullards. "But it isn't. This involves more than a few truckloads of fruit. It involves a whole corporation. I have a boss of my own I have to answer to." He sighed. "I don't make the rules, friends, I only follow them. If it was strictly up to me, I'd open those gates in a second."

"No, you wouldn't." Atwater stared at the ground. "Because you're a prick."

"Pardon me, gentlemen, but I've had about enough of this," Saunders said as he brushed past them. "It's been a long day, and I am going home."

The drivers made no move to block him. They stood there in a stunned pack and railed about the harshness of their treatment, but their hands were tied. They had no means of appeal, so they returned to their trucks, swung them around, and drove away, everybody except Atwater, who was unable to summon the energy to leave. He dozed some more in his cab and woke again in the middle of the night. The moon was low in the sky, and he got out and felt how hot the air still was. He stood on a tire and reached up into the gondola to taste a grape. As he expected, the skin was puckered, and it was way too sweet. The same thing was true of every other grape he tasted. All his work, all his striving, had come down to this—a roll of the dice and boom! Snake eyes.

A first streak of dawn light showed on the horizon. Soon workers who'd been tossed unceremoniously from their beds after a few hours of sleep began arriving at the winery again, unlocking the big gates and hosing down the concrete floors, padding around in rubber boots as they racked yesterday's juice and measured the juice already in their tanks to calibrate its relative acidity and the level of its residual sugar.

At seven o'clock, Atwater pulled up to the sugar shack and lifted his battered and dejected face to Rawley Kimball, who had his clipboard in his good hand and was scribbling away on it.

"Hey there, Arthur!" Kimball yelled to him in a chipper way. "Ain't you the early bird!"

"It's because I was the goddam late bird yesterday," Atwater said, convinced now that the fault was at least half his. "That prick Wade Saunders closed me out."

"Oh, I am sorry to hear that." Kimball sounded honestly concerned.

"Not nearly as sorry as I am, Rawley."

A tester stepped to the platform and went through the usual routine. Atwater awaited a verdict that he already knew in advance. He watched the tester run the sample through a grape press and catch the juice in a bucket before sinking a refractometer into it.

"Cabernet?" the tester asked.

"That's right."

The tester left the platform, and Kimball came back out after a little while. Atwater ignored the Brix number scribbled on the slip of paper Kimball gave him.

"Those grapes turned on you in the night," Kimball told him. "What you've got there now is damaged goods."

"I'm aware of that," Atwater said.

"I don't like to downgrade you, Arthur, but I have to. Your grapes aren't good for much, except maybe our low-end jug wines. That's B-grade fruit."

"I'll go dump the load inside."

"Listen," Kimball said to him with some urgency. "I feel real bad about this. I know how hard you worked."

"Thank you, Rawley."

"It's unfair, and I know it. But it happens to a few growers every year. It's part of the game. Sometimes it's just your turn to go through it. I still feel real bad for you, though."

Atwater smiled. "Did you say 'unfair'?"

"I did."

"That's what I thought you said."

He stuffed the paper into a pocket and got back in his cab. The truck stuttered forward, and he weighed in, dumped his grapes, and weighed out. The difference was about eighteen tons. According to the CV contract, B-grade fruit went for $100 less per ton than A-grade fruit, so that represented an $1,800 loss for Victor Torelli right there, to which Atwater would have to add the extra money he was paying his pickers, another $75 dollars or so a day for about three more weeks—he figured his mistake had cost the old man five grand, or somewhere near it. Torelli would not be pleased. Again, Atwater had let him down.

The crew was already picking at the farm when he drove up, and he spoke to Manuel and put him formally in charge, while he, Atwater, the boss, ran some errands—that was how he phrased it, anyhow. Then he took off in his Jeep without changing his funky clothes and bought a torpedo sandwich, some potato chips, and a six-pack of beer at Roy's. He had polished off all but one of the beers way before noon and began to entertain a sudden and highly irrational notion that happiness in this life might yet be his. He was about a hundred miles from Carson Valley at the time and traveling steadily north. In Laytonville, he stopped at a loggers' bar for a shot of whiskey and drank three shots instead, thinking that he ought to check into a motel and get some sleep, but in fact his forehead was soon resting on the mahogany bar, and he slept like that into the early afternoon.

My Country

Leonore Wilson

"There are roads to take when you think of your country."
                                        —Muriel Rukeyser

And what if I witness but do not choose,
if I merely drive by, pull back
thinking of the one and only, if I am that
complacent to the woman with the purple bruises
around her neck, scourged neck, crown
of the black and blue. Christ
I see her weeping next to the oversized tattooed
drunk of a man. And what if I choose
not to aid her stalled U-haul, overheated
smoking machine of the underworld, near
where the wild irises bloom their white flags
from the red soil, where the unnameable

General in his nineteenth century bliss
shot one of the last Wappos from paradise.
And what if I choose not to aid her,
an entire life stuffed in the truck's
caraspace, what if I drive by
keeping my thumb in my book
because I am terrified, made numb
and dumb as the virgin girl
when the word made flesh entered her,
when the ordinary mud swallow sang,
dove hollowed out, she who was asleep,
daydreaming, preferring the milk of the cathedral,
girl who knew there are blue abrasions
in the meadows, that light could scald;
she who knew men with eyes in their chests,
slobs, dogs, big babies smoking pipes.
What if I drive by, choosing to look
the other way, mother, wife,
because it is spring in my country
and in spring it is easier to be ignorant, unaccountable,
then what, then who will stop, then who.

The Orchards

I learned the body first,
scrambling under wire
kneading the black earth
with my fists as if

to get it right, as if I
were hoofing the furrows,
spreading the scoured seed.
Under the saplings,
under the parental trees,
near the one-room schoolhouse,
the heavy pears
of summer were plump as textbooks,
the traffic savage
and in waves; convertibles
and boats with their tops down,
teenagers shouting
like mischievous geese
everywhere.
I resolved to die to you
there under the clear sky
of my motherland.
Love was unglamourous
and quick
as you
unburied me like gold
under trunks, rolled me
from shade
to sun, the dried out
ears of wheat bruised under my belly,
the stubborn foxtails, oats,
little fangs of thistles.
And afterwards
we'd eat the fruit
that had fallen as though
it were left for us; the milk-white
meat like wine.

In the orchards, I learned
god wanted us
nurtured, forgiven;
he showed us there
we could have it
again
that world unbroken,
all pliant and rich
with desire.

Wine Grapes for Breakfast

Jane Hirshfield

Sweet
at first
on the tongue,
hours later
the red grapes
still sting,
as if trying
to speak of something—
what the hook

---

tells the fish
perhaps,
or the wand
or stick hears
before conductor
or mule driver
brings it down.

May's Lion

Ursula Le Guin

Jim remembers it as a bobcat, and he was May's nephew, and ought to know. It probably was a bobcat. I don't think May would have changed her story, though you can't trust a good storyteller not to make the story suit herself, or get the facts to fit the story better. Anyhow she told it to us more than once, because my mother and I would ask for it; and the way I remember it, it was a mountain lion. And the way I remember May telling it is sitting on the edge of the irrigation tank we used to swim in, cement rough as a lava flow and hot in the sun, the long cracks tarred over. She was an old lady then with a long Irish upper lip, kind and wary and balky. She liked to come sit and talk with my mother while I swam; she didn't have all that many people to talk to. She always had chickens, in the chickenhouse very near the back door of the farmhouse, so the whole place smelled pretty strong of chickens, and as long as she could she kept a cow or two down in the old barn by the creek. The first of May's cows I remember was Pearl, a big, handsome Holstein who gave fourteen or twenty-four or forty gallons or quarts of milk at a milking, whichever is right for a prize milker. Pearl was beautiful in my eyes when I was four or five years old; I loved and admired her. I remember how excited I was, how I reached upward to them, when Pearl or the workhorse Prince, for whom my love amounted to worship, would put an immense and sensitive muzzle through the three-strand fence to whisk a cornhusk from my fearful hand; and then the munching and the sweet breath and the big nose would be at the barbed wire again: the offering is acceptable....After Pearl there was Rosie, a purebred Jersey. May got her either cheap or free because she was a runt calf, so tiny that May brought her home on her lap in the back of the car, like a fawn. And Rosie always looked like she had some deer in her. She was a lovely, clever little cow and even more willful than old May. She often chose not to come in to be milked. We would hear May calling and then see her trudging across our lower pasture with the bucket, going to find Rosie wherever Rosie had decided to be milked today on the wild hills she had to roam in, a hundred acres of our and Old Jim's land. Then May had a fox terrier named Pinky, who yipped and nipped and turned me against fox terriers for life, but he was long gone when the mountain lion came; and the black cats who lived in the barn kept discreetly out of the story. As a matter of fact, now I think of it, the chickens weren't in it either. It might have been quite different if they had been. May had quit keeping chickens after old Mrs. Walter died. It was just her all alone there, and Rosie and the cats down in the barn and nobody else within sight or sound of the old farm. We were in our house up the hill only in the summer, and Jim lived in town, those years. What time of year it was I don't know, but I imagine the grass still green or just turning gold. And May was in the house, in the kitchen, where she lived entirely unless she was asleep or outdoors, when she heard this noise.

Now you need May herself, sitting skinny on the edge of the irrigation tank, seventy or eighty or ninety years old, nobody knew how old May was and she had made sure they couldn't find out, opening her pleated lips and letting out this noise—a huge, awful yowl, starting soft with a nasal hum and rising slowly into a snarling gargle that sank away into a sobbing purr....It got better every time she told the story.

"It was some meow," she said.

So she went to the kitchen door, opened it, and looked out. Then she shut the kitchen door and went to the kitchen window to look out, because there was a mountain lion under the fig tree.

Puma, cougar, catamount; *Felis concolor,* the shy, secret, shadowy lion of the New World, four or five feet long plus a yard of black-tipped tail, weighs about what a woman weighs, lives where the deer live from Canada to Chile, but always shyer, always fewer, the color of dry leaves, dry grass.

There were plenty of deer in the Valley in the forties, but no mountain lion had been seen for decades anywhere near where people lived. Maybe way back up in the canyons; but Jim, who hunted and knew every deer-trail in the hills, had never seen a lion. Nobody had, except May, now, alone in her kitchen.

"I thought maybe it was sick," she told us. "It wasn't acting right. I don't think a lion would walk right into the yard like that if it was feeling well. If I'd still had the chickens it'd be a different story maybe! But it just walked around some, and then it lay down there," and she points between the fig tree and the decrepit garage. "And then after a while it kind of meowed again, and got up and come into the shade right there." The fig tree, planted when the house was built, about the time May was born, makes a great, green, sweet-smelling shade. "It just laid there looking around. It wasn't well," says May.

She had lived with and looked after animals all her life; she had also earned her living for years as a nurse.

"Well, I didn't know exactly what to do for it. So I put out some water for it. It didn't even get up when I come out the door. I put the water down there, not so close to it that we'd scare each other, see, and it kept watching me, but it didn't move. After I went back in, it did get up and tried to drink some water. Then it made that kind of meowowow. I do believe it come here because it was looking for help. Or just for company, maybe."

The afternoon went on, May in the kitchen, the lion under the fig tree.

But down in the barnyard by the creek was Rosie the cow. Fortunately the gate was shut, so she could not come wandering up to the house and meet the lion; but she would be needing to be milked, come six or seven o'clock, and that got to worrying May. She also worried how long a sick mountain lion might hang around, keeping her shut in the house. May didn't like being shut in.

"I went out a time or two, and went shoo!"

Eyes shining amidst fine wrinkles, she flaps her thin arms at the lion. "Shoo! Go on home now!"

But the silent wild creature watches her with yellow eyes and does not stir.

"So when I was talking to Miss Macy on the telephone, she said it might have rabies, and I ought to call the sheriff. I was uneasy then. So finally I did that, and they come out, those county police, you know. Two carloads."

Her voice is dry and quiet.

"I guess there was nothing else they knew how to do. So they shot it."

She looks off across the field Old Jim, her brother, used to plow with Prince the horse and irrigate with the water from this tank. Now wild oats and blackberry grow there. In another thirty years it will be a rich man's vineyard, a tax write-off.

"He was seven feet long, all stretched out, before they took him off. And so thin! They all said, 'Well, Aunt May, I guess you were scared there! I guess you were some scared!' But I wasn't. I didn't want him shot. But I didn't know what to do for him. And I did need to get to Rosie."

I have told this true story which May gave to us as truly as I could, and now I want to tell it as fiction, yet without taking it from her: rather to give it back to her, if I can do so. It is a tiny part of the history of the Valley, and I want to make it part of the Valley outside history. Now the field that the poor man plowed and the rich man harvested lies on the edge of a little town, houses and workshops of timber and fieldstone standing among almond, oak, and eucalyptus trees; and now May is an old woman with a name that means the month of May: Rains End. An old woman with a long, wrinkled-pleated upper lip, she is living alone for the summer in her summer place, a meadow a mile or so up in the hills above the little town. Sinshan. She took her cow Rose with her, and since Rose tends to wander she keeps her on a long tether down by the tiny creek, and moves her into fresh grass now and then. The summerhouse is what they call a nine-pole house, a mere frame of poles stuck in the ground—one of them is a live digger-pine sapling—with stick and matting walls, and mat roof and floors. It doesn't rain in the dry season, and the roof is just for shade. But the house and its little front yard where Rains End has her camp stove and clay oven and matting loom are well shaded by a fig tree that was planted there a hundred years or so ago by her grandmother.

Rains End herself has no grandchildren; she never bore a child, and her one or two marriages were brief and very long ago. She has a nephew and two grandnieces, and feels herself an aunt to all children, even when they are afraid of her and rude to her because she has got so ugly with old age, smelling as musty as a chickenhouse. She considers it natural for children to shrink away from somebody part way dead, and knows that when they're a little older and have got used to her they'll ask her for stories. She was for sixty years a member of the Doctors Lodge, and though she doesn't do curing anymore, people still ask her to help with nursing sick children, and the children come to long for the kind, authoritative touch of her hands when she bathes them to bring a fever down, or changes a dressing, or combs out bed-tangled hair with witch hazel and great patience.

So Rains End was just waking up from an early afternoon nap in the heat of the day, under the matting roof, when she heard a noise, a huge, awful yowl that started soft with a nasal hum and rose slowly into a snarling gargle that sank away into a sobbing purr....And she got up and looked out from the open side of the house of sticks and matting, and saw a mountain lion under the fig tree. She looked at him from her house; he looked at her from his.

And this part of the story is much the same: the old woman; the lion; and, down by the creek, the cow.

It was hot. Crickets sang shrill in the yellow grass on all the hills and canyons, in all the chaparral. Rains End filled a bowl with water from an unglazed jug and came slowly out of the house. Halfway between the house and the lion, she set the bowl down on the dirt. She turned and went back to the house.

The lion got up after a while and came and sniffed at the water. He lay down again with a soft, querulous groan, almost like a sick child, and looked at Rains End with the yellow eyes that saw her in a different way than she had ever been seen before.

She sat on the matting in the shade of the open part of her house and did some mending. When she looked up at the lion she sang under her breath, tunelessly; she wanted to remember the Puma Dance Song but could only remember bits of it, so she made a song for the occasion:

You are there, lion.

You are there, lion....

As the afternoon wore on she began to worry about going down
to milk Rose. Unmilked, the cow would start tugging at her tether
and making a commotion. That was likely to upset the lion. He lay so
close to the house now that if she came out that too might upset him,
and she did not want to frighten him or to become frightened of him.
He had evidently come for some reason, and it behoved her to find
out what the reason was. Probably he was sick; his coming so close to
a human person was strange, and people who behave strangely are
usually sick or in some kind of pain. Sometimes, though, they are
spiritually moved to act strangely. The lion might be a messenger, or
might have some message of his own for her or her townspeople. She
was more used to seeing birds as messengers; the four-footed people
go about their own business. But the lion, dweller in the Seventh
House, comes from the place dreams come from. Maybe she did not
understand. Maybe someone else would understand. She could go
over and tell Valiant and her family, whose summerhouse was in
Gahheya meadow, farther up the creek; or she could go over to
Buck's, on Baldy Knoll. But there were four or five adolescents there,
and one of them might come and shoot the lion, to boast that he'd
saved old Rains End from getting clawed to bits and eaten.

Mooooooo! said Rose, down by the creek, reproachfully.

The sun was still above the southwest ridge, but the branches of
pines were across it, and the heavy heat was out of it, and shadows
were welling up in the low fields of wild oats and blackberry.

Mooooooo! said Rose again, louder.

The lion lifted up his square, heavy head, the color of dry wild
oats, and gazed down across the pastures. Rains End knew from that
weary movement that he was very ill. He had come for company in
dying, that was all.

"I'll come back, lion," Rains End sang tunelessly. "Lie still. Be
quiet. I'll come back soon." Moving softly and easily, as she would

move in a room with a sick child, she got her milking pail and stool, slung the stool on her back with a woven strap so as to leave a hand free, and came out of the house. The lion watched her, at first very tense, the yellow eyes firing up for a moment, but then put his head down again with that little grudging, groaning sound. "I'll come back, lion," Rains End said. She went down to the creekside and milked a nervous and indignant cow. Rose could smell lion, and demanded in several ways, all eloquent, just what Rains End intended to *do?* Rains End ignored her questions and sang milking songs to her: "Su bonny, su bonny, be still my grand cow…" Once she had to slap her hard on the hip. "Quit that, you old fool! Get over! I am *not* going to untie you and have you walking into trouble! I won't let him come down this way."

She did not say how she planned to stop him.

She retethered Rose where she could stand down in the creek if she liked. When she came back up the rise with the pail of milk in hand, the lion had not moved. The sun was down, the air above the ridges turning clear gold. The yellow eyes watched her, no light in them. She came to pour milk into the lion's bowl. As she did so, he all at once half rose up. Rains End started, and spilled some of the milk she was pouring. "Shoo! Stop that!" she whispered fiercely, waving her skinny arm at the lion. "Lie down now! I'm afraid of you when you get up, can't you see that, stupid? Lie down now, lion. There you are. Here I am. It's all right. You know what you're doing." Talking softly as she went, she returned to her house of stick and matting. There she sat down as before, in the open porch, on the grass mats.

The mountain lion made the grumbling sound, ending with a long sigh, and let his head sink back down on his paws.

Rains End got some cornbread and a tomato from the pantry box while there was still daylight left to see by, and ate slowly and neatly. She did not offer the lion food. He had not touched the milk, and she thought he would eat no more in the House of Earth.

From time to time as the quiet evening darkened and stars gathered thicker overhead she sang to the lion. She sang the five songs of *Going Westward to the Sunrise,* which are sung to human beings dying. She did not know if it was proper and appropriate to sing these songs to a dying mountain lion, but she did not know his songs.

Twice he also sang: once a quavering moan, like a house cat challenging another tom to battle, and once a long, sighing purr.

Before the Scorpion had swung clear of Sinshan Mountain, Rains End had pulled her heavy shawl around herself in case the fog came in, and had gone sound asleep in the porch of her house.

She woke with the grey light before sunrise. The lion was a motionless shadow, a little farther from the trunk of the fig tree than he had been the night before. As the light grew, she saw that he had stretched himself out full length. She knew he had finished his dying, and sang the fifth song, the last song, in a whisper, for him:

The doors of the Four Houses
are open.
Surely they are open.

Near sunrise she went to milk Rose and to wash in the creek. When she came back up to the house she went closer to the lion, though not so close as to crowd him, and stood for a long time looking at him stretched out in the long, tawny, delicate light. "As thin as I am!" she said to Valiant, when she went up to Gahheya later in the morning to tell the story and to ask help carrying the body of the lion off where the buzzards and coyotes could clean it.

It's still your story, Aunt May; it was your lion. He came to you. He brought his death to you, a gift; but the men with the guns won't take gifts, they think they own death already. And so they took from you the honor he did you, and you felt that loss. I wanted to restore it. But you don't need it. You followed the lion where he went, years ago now.

◾ Author Biographies

BILL BARICH (1943–) is the author of five books, including *Laughing in the Hills* (1980), *Traveling Light* (1984), *Hard to be Good* (1987), *Big Dreams* (1994), and *Carson Valley* (1997). He lives in the San Francisco Bay Area.

AMBROSE BIERCE (1842–1914?) was a major in the Union army for five years. After his release, he began writing the vitriolic works that made him famous, including *The Devil's Dictionary* (1906) and *Can Such Things Be?* (1893). Turning his back on America, at the end of his life he went to Mexico to seek the "good, kind darkness."

KATE BRAVERMAN (1950–) is the winner of two Best American Short Story Awards and the O. Henry Award. She has written two collections of short stories, *Squandering the Blue* (1990) and *Small Craft Warnings* (1998), as well as four poetry collections and a trilogy of novels about Los Angeles. She lives in a remote area of the Allegheny Mountains, New York.

DAVID BROMIGE (1933–) was Poet-In-Residence at Sonoma State University from 1970–1993. The winner of numerous awards and honors, he is the author of thirty books, including *Tight Corners* (1974), *My Poetry* (1980), *Desire* (1988), *Men, Women & Vehicles* (1990), *Harbormaster of Hong Kong* (1993), and *A Cast of Tens* (1994). He lives in Sebastopol.

DOROTHY BRYANT (1930–), a native San Franciscan, received a B.A. in music and an M.A. in creative writing from San Francisco State University. Since 1960, she has published twelve books, including *Confessions of Madame Psyche* (1986), which won the American Book Award. She lives in Berkeley.

JAMES CONAWAY (1941–) was born in Memphis and came to California in 1963, when he received the Wallace Stegner Creative Writing Fellowship at Stanford University. An accomplished journalist, he is the author of *The Big Easy* (1970), *Judge: The Life and Times of Leander Perez* (1973), *The Texans* (1976), *Napa* (1990), and *Memphis Afternoons* (1993).

GEORGE HORATIO DERBY (1823–1861) graduated from West Point in 1846. Three years later, he came to California to conduct military expeditions into the gold country and the San Joaquin Valley. Under the pseudonyms "Squibob" and "John Phoenix," he published dozens of wildly popular sketches in the *San Diego Herald* and San Francisco's *Pioneer*. A collection of his writings, *Phoenixiana,* was published in 1855.

PHILIP DOW (1937–) was raised in Vallejo and Napa, where he currently lives. His work has appeared regularly in magazines and in anthologies, including *The American Poetry Anthology, Best Poems of 1976,* and *Quickly Aging Here.* He is also the author of *Paying Back the Sea* (1979) and the editor of *19 New American Poets of the Golden Gate* (1984).

M.F.K. FISHER (1908–1992) is best known for her writings about food and cooking, including such works as *How to Cook a Wolf* (1942), *The Gastronomical Me* (1943), and *The Art of Eating* (1954). An advocate for the simple pleasures of good food and wine, her writing is largely autobiographical. She lived and wrote in the Napa Valley for many years, even after she was bedridden from Parkinson's disease at the end of her life.

HILDEGARDE FLANNER (1899–1987) spent most of her life in California, writing essays, plays, and poems, and working extensively with conservation groups. She first came to California from Indiana in 1919 to attend U.C. Berkeley, and eventually settled in Southern California. In 1962, she moved to Calistoga with her family, where she lived until her death.

JANE HIRSHFIELD (1953–) graduated from Princeton University in 1973. Afterwards, she studied for eight years at the San Francisco Zen Center. An award-winning poet and translator, she is the author of *Alaya* (1982), *Of Gravity & Angels* (1988), *The October Palace* (1994), *The Lives of the Heart* (1997), and *Nine Gates: Essays on Poetry* (1997). She currently lives in Marin.

SIDNEY HOWARD (1891–1939) was born in Oakland. He began writing plays while on the editorial staff of *Life,* winning the Pulitzer Prize in 1925 for *They Knew What They Wanted.* He went on to write many popular dramas, including the screenplay of *Gone With the Wind,* for which he was awarded a posthumous Oscar in 1940.

IDWAL JONES (1890–1964) began his literary career as a book reviewer for the *San Francisco Chronicle.* During his lifetime, he wrote over 200 articles on California geology, folklore, history, mining, and viticulture. His numerous works include *The Vineyard* (1942), *High Bonnet,* (1945), *Vermilion* (1947), and *Vines in the Sun* (1949).

URSULA LE GUIN (1929–) was born in Berkeley. Educated at Radcliffe College and Columbia University, she is known primarily as a writer of science fiction and fantasy. Her novels, poems, and essays have received critical praise and numerous honors, including the Nebula Award, the Hugo Award, and the National Book Award. She lives in Portland, Oregon.

JACK LONDON (1876–1916) was raised in a depressed part of Oakland, the illegitimate son of an astrologer and a spirit medium. Although he briefly attended U.C. Berkeley, he was largely self-educated, working as a Yukon miner, a sailor on a whaling ship, and an oyster pirate. After breaking onto the literary scene in 1903 with *The Call of the Wild,* he made his permanent home, physically and intellectually, in Sonoma. He went on to write such favorites as *White Fang* (1906) and *Martin Eden* (1909).

FRANCES MARION (1886–1973) grew up in San Francisco. She wrote hundreds of screenplays over the course of her life, becoming one of Hollywood's most prominent screenwriters. She won an Academy Award for Best Screenplay in 1930 for *The Big House,* and again in 1931 for *The Champ.* In addition to *Valley People* (1935), she also authored seven books.

JOHN MCPHEE (1931–) was educated at Princeton University and Cambridge University. He has carved a unique literary niche for himself, writing about specialized subjects—including geology, agriculture, and anthropology—for the lay reader. He was born and raised in Princeton, New Jersey, where he currently lives.

JANE MEAD (1958–) is a native of Baltimore, but has spent extensive time in the Napa Valley, where her family has been growing Zinfandel since 1913. Her work has appeared regularly in journals, newspapers, and anthologies, including the *American Poetry Review, The New York Times,* and *Best American Poetry of 1990.* The recipient of a Whiting Writers' Award, she is currently Poet-in-Residence at Wake Forest University.

SIR GEORGE SIMPSON (1787-1860) was a Scotsman who rose through the ranks of England's Hudson's Bay Company. He was eventually named governor of the company's vast holdings in Canada, where his diminutive stature and ruthless character soon gained him the nickname "Little Emperor." While on a round-the-world tour in 1841, he visited California to determine whether to invest the company's resources in what was then Mexican land with an uncertain future.

ROBERT LOUIS STEVENSON (1850–1894) was born in Edinburgh, Scotland, and was educated as an engineer. An essayist and poet, he is probably best known for his classic adventure story, *Treasure Island*. In 1880, he spent the summer honeymooning with his American bride in the Napa Valley, where he began writing *The Silverado Squatters* (1883).

BAYARD TAYLOR (1825–1878) achieved instant celebrity in 1846 with *Views-A-Foot,* an account of his two-year walking trip through Europe. He first came to Napa in 1949 while covering the Gold Rush for Horace Greeley's *New York Tribune,* and his sketches from this period were published as *El Dorado* in 1850. *At Home and Abroad* is composed of his works from a later trip to California.

JESSAMYN WEST (1902–1984) grew up in Whittier, California. Although she is best known for her short stories, her work has included fiction, nonfiction, poetry, and screenplays. One of her most popular story collections, *The Friendly Persuasion* (1945), was made into a film starring Gary Cooper. *To See the Dream,* the earliest of several nonfiction memoirs, grew out of a journal she kept while living in Napa and working on the screen adaptation for the film.

LEONORE WILSON (1958–) lives with her family on a cattle ranch in the east hills of the Napa Valley. Her work has appeared in such magazines as *Quarterly West, Poet and Critic, Laurel Review, California Quarterly,* and *Yellow Silk*. She was nominated for a Pushcart Prize in 1997. She currently teaches creative writing at Napa Valley College and is working on her poetry book, *Amado.*